OPEN WATER SWIMMING

Penny Lee Dean, EdD

Holder of 13
Open Water Swimming World Records

International Swimming
Hall of Fame, 1996

Human Kinetics

Library of Congress Cataloging-in-Publication Data

Dean, Penny Lee, 1955-
    Open water swimming / Penny Lee Dean.
        p.   cm.
    Includes bibliographical references (p.) and index.
    ISBN 0-88011-704-4
    1. Long distance swimming.   I. Title.
    GV838.53.L65D43   1998
    797.2'1--dc21
                                          97-38472
                                          CIP

ISBN: 0-88011-704-4

Acquisitions Editor: Ken Mange; **Developmental Editor:** Julie Rhoda; **Assistant Editors:** Sandra Merz Bott, Cassandra Mitchell, and John Wentworth; **Editorial Assistant:** Laura T. Seversen; **Copyeditor:** Cinci Stowell; **Proofreader:** Sarah Wiseman; **Indexer:** Theresa Schaefer; **Graphic Designer:** Robert Reuther; **Graphic Artist:** Sandra Meier; **Photo Manager:** Boyd LaFoon; **Cover Designer:** Jack Davis; **Photographer (cover):** The Stock Market/Michael Kevin Daly; **Photographer (interior):** Photos on pages 2, 4, 8, 20, 50, 55, 92, 156, 164, 166 by Human Kinetics/Tom Roberts; **Illustrators:** Keith Blomberg and M.R. Greenberg; **Printer:** United Graphics

Human Kinetics books are available at special discounts for bulk purchase. Special editions or book excerpts can also be created to specification. For details, contact the Special Sales Manager at Human Kinetics.

Printed in the United States of America

10   9   8   7   6   5   4   3   2

Human Kinetics
Web site: www.humankinetics.com

United States: Human Kinetics, P.O. Box 5076, Champaign, IL 61825-5076
800-747-4457
e-mail: humank@hkusa.com

Canada: Human Kinetics, 475 Devonshire Road Unit 100, Windsor, ON N8Y 2L5
800-465-7301 (in Canada only)
e-mail: orders@hkcanada.com

Europe: Human Kinetics, Units C2/C3 Wira Business Park, West Park Ring Road
Leeds LS16 6EB, United Kingdom
+44 (0) 113 278 1708
e-mail: hk@hkeurope.com

Australia: Human Kinetics, 57A Price Avenue, Lower Mitcham, South Australia 5062
08 8277 1555
e-mail: liahka@senet.com.au

New Zealand: Human Kinetics, P.O. Box 105-231, Auckland Central
09-523-3462
e-mail: hkp@ihug.co.nz

Contents

Preface . . . . *v*

Acknowledgments . . . . *vii*

Chapter 1 **The Lure of Open Water** 1

Find out what drives swimmers to pursue open water events—whether it's the appeal of successfully conquering the elements or challenging the mind and body to their limits.

Chapter 2 **Safety in the Water World** 7

Swimming safely is vital to your success in the open water. Learn how to be ready for any situation—from preventing hypothermia to watching the weather.

Chapter 3 **Equipment for the Open Water** 29

Suit up for your event with the right swimsuit or wet suit, goggles, and more. Learn what you'll need to pack for race day or for longer swims, and how to choose and equip your support craft.

Chapter 4 **The Shortest Distance Between Start and Finish** 46

Navigating efficiently is essential for your best swim. Learn visual techniques to help you reach the finish faster as well as the basics of craft-assisted navigation for longer events.

Chapter 5 **Technique Tips for the Open Water** . . 67

Improve the speed, efficiency, and endurance of your stroke with stroke drills and numerous tips for adapting your stroke and kick for the open water.

Chapter 6 **Training for Faster Swims** 91

Tailor your complete training program to include weight training and calisthenics as well as swim training. This chapter guides you through developing your seasonal plan to the details of your daily workouts.

Chapter 7 **Training Your Mind** **137**

Learn proven motivation, relaxation, and affirmation techniques to help you focus on your goals and maintain a positive attitude throughout training and competition.

Chapter 8 **Race Tactics** **153**

Whether you're a triathlete or a marathon swimmer, planning your race tactics can ensure success. Discover how to master your start, swim safely in a crowd, pace for your race, and draft and drag legally.

Chapter 9 **Final Preparation** **169**

You're ready to race—find out the best time to start your taper, to shave down, and what to eat before you swim to ensure your best race.

Chapter 10 **Major Events** **197**

Looking for an open water swimming event or triathlon to try? Check out this contact information for swimming and triathlon organizations as well as some major international events.

Appendix *216*

Bibliography *217*

Index *218*

About the Author *223*

Preface

In the last 23 years, every major open water swimming record has been broken. Many of these records were shattered by an hour to an hour and a half. Why did this happen? A new breed of open water swimmers left the pool with the attitude of swimming quickly, not just succeeding or surviving a long distance swim. In addition, swimmers began to experiment with and refine changes in nutrition, navigation, mental training, and the actual physical training for open water swims.

During the 1970s, an open water swimmer who wanted a tougher challenge initiated the triathlon. He decided to combine an open water swim with a long-distance bike ride and a run. The immediate popularity of this athletic endeavor was amazing. Initially, 5 to 20 people entered the early triathlons. Most triathlons today have hundreds of entrants. The Ironman in Hawaii has grown so much that a lottery was begun with thousands of entrants to allow 100 extra triathletes to compete in the event. In addition, more triathletes are entering open water races to improve their swimming, aiding the growth of both sports. Within 30 years of its inception, the triathlon event will be held in the 2000 Olympics in Sydney, Australia.

Open Water Swimming not only teaches a beginning open water swimmer or triathlete every aspect of swimming in open water, but can also teach the experienced triathlete, long distance (1 mile to 16 miles), and marathon (over 16 miles) swimmer the nuances of faster and more efficient swimming in open water. This book provides information on how to plan for a race from .5 to 50 miles in a lake, a river, or the ocean and for more than one race in a season.

Chapters explore open water safety, equipment, navigation, stroke technique, race tactics, mental preparation, nourishment, tapering, and race-day guidelines. In addition, chapters discuss the differences involved in swimming long distance and marathon swims, as well as the specific needs of a triathlete during the swimming portion of short, international, Olympic, long, Ironman, and ultra distance triathlons. Thus, this book functions as a detailed training guide for the whole range of open water swimmers who are emerging today.

Throughout the text, I recount many noteworthy and exciting open water swims and races for motivational and historical perspective. For example, the book describes in horrifying detail how 101 swimmers entered the chilly waters off Catalina in January, 1927, to race across the 21-mile channel to have only one finish, 17-year-old George Young of Canada, who became the first individual to swim the Catalina Channel. This swim began the annual assault of the Catalina Channel by numerous athletes. Since 1927, over 113 swims have succeeded.

I also profile some of the best open water swimmers and triathletes from the beginning of both sports and for all distances. These exciting profiles explore the courage each athlete demonstrated, the dangerous encounters some experienced, and the perseverance each needed to continue in a race or swim. For example, as a young open water swimmer, Chad Hundeby won the 10-mile U.S. nationals and qualified for the U.S. national team. Later that year, the U.S. team was attempting a relay across the Catalina Channel. Chad should have swum first since he was the fastest swimmer; however, his fear prevented him from swimming at night. Chad had to swim sixth on the relay. Chad was terrified of sharks and marine life. As his coach, I decided not to push him to deal with his fears at this point. In the next three years, under my auspices as the U.S. national coach, Chad overcame these fears and won the first World 25K Championships in Australia. He went on to become the world professional champion for many years and even broke my 17-year overall world record for swimming the English Channel.

Each story portrays the personal satisfaction you can receive from conquering your fears, whether your aspirations lie in an open water swim or a triathlon. Both are lonely sports that ask athletes to push themselves to their limits, as they conquer the challenges of the ever-changing weather conditions, tides, currents, hypothermia, heat stroke, marine life, and loneliness to realize their dreams.

Acknowledgments

This project was a combined effort with family and friends. My mother, Frances Dean, not only read the book numerous times, but also helped extensively with editing. I would like to thank my other readers, Toni Fernandez, Pete Huisveld, and Dale Petranech. Each dedicated numerous hours to the project's success. In addition, I would like to thank Pete Huisveld for writing the navigation section on the GPS system and his adaptation to it. Finally, I would like to thank Claudia Klaver for encouraging and supporting me throughout the process of writing this book.

1

The Lure of Open Water

In 1987, Lynne Cox of Southern California decided to swim the Bering Strait from the Little Diomede Island off of the United States to Big Diomede in the Soviet Union. Lynne had already swum the English and Catalina Channels in record times and the Cook Strait in New Zealand, and was the first person to swim around the Cape of Good Hope in South Africa, Strait of Magellan in Chile, and numerous other swims around the world. She wanted to bridge the two cold-war nations through a swim for peace. This dangerous and challenging swim across the Bering Strait was 2.7 miles in water ranging from 40 to 48 degrees F and one that no one had ever attempted. Lynne not only had to acquire State Department approval from the U.S. and Russia, she had to gather experts in currents, hypothermia, and cold-water immersion to assist in her swim.

On August 7 Lynne became the first person to cross the frigid water in two hours and six minutes. Her core temperature was not affected by the cold water; in fact, it increased, baffling all the researchers. Her 30 to 35 percent body fat kept her warm in the water, but once she left the water and walked up the beach, her temperature dropped significantly, and she experienced the initial stages of hypothermia. An open water swimmer has to be warmed quickly and monitored long after a swim to ensure safety. Lynne was driven to do a swim never attempted by anyone else,

in dangerous conditions; it was the challenge and the lure of open water swimming that inspired her.

WHAT IS OPEN WATER SWIMMING?

Open water swimming, by definition, means a swim in any natural body of water—river, lake, or ocean. This book will focus on long distance and marathon distance swims and each of the six triathlon distances. For competitions and record setting, open water swimming is divided into short distance, long distance, and marathon swimming. Short distance swimming is any distance under 1.5 K (about 1 mile). Long distance swimming is any distance from 1.5 K (about 1 mile) up to 25 K (16 miles). Marathon swimming is all swims over 25 K (16 miles) or a swim lasting over 5 hours. The swim portions of triathlons are divided into short (.25 to .50 miles), international (.5 to 1.25 miles), Olympic (1.5K), long (1.25 to 2.5 miles), Ironman (2.4 miles), and ultra distances (over 2 miles). Completing a swim, regardless of the distance, is the goal that draws many open water swimmers into the sport. This goal is more important to the swimmer than the time taken to complete the event, since Mother Nature is in charge of the elements.

CONQUERING THE ELEMENTS

Lynne Cox accomplished one of the most difficult swims in open water history. Why would she pit herself against rough currents and frigid water? Competing with the elements is the challenge of open water swimming. No one can control Mother Nature; the weather, water temperature, currents, and tides can make a relatively easy swim dangerous and even life threatening. This "unknown" is what an open water swimmer challenges.

ACCEPTING THE CHALLENGE

Open water swimmers have to push themselves through numerous pain walls. Some days conditions may be perfect, but your mind may not be ready to face the solitude, mental stress, or physical pain of the swim. Your support crew may not even know this battle is going on within you. At other times, your body may give out. So why do this to yourself? Because, if you have ever battled and persevered through formidable obstacles to achieve a goal, you know the indescribable exhilaration of success. You feel as if you can conquer anything in life if you just fight through the barriers. This feeling is why open water swimmers keep challenging the elements.

ACCOMPLISHING YOUR GOALS

The enchantment of looking across to a distant shore lures open water swimmers to swim across. Standing on the English shore peering toward the French coast or experiencing the vastness of Lake Tahoe entices you. You want to know if you can make it. Although you might not be the first to cross, you can add your name to the record books. Whether you achieve a record or not, just finishing the swim successfully is reward enough to make the attempt.

Alison Streeter is not a fast swimmer, but she has endurance. Since 1982 she has swum the English Channel an unprecedented 36 times. This is more than any other man or woman. Why swim

it so many times? To Alison, the question has always been, "why not?" She has not let the cold water, unpredictable weather, dangerous tides and currents, oil slicks, jellyfish, hundreds of boats, or seaweed bother her. She may not ever win a race, but she has her own set of challenges and conquers them. This attitude exemplifies the lure of open water swimming.

When I was 10 years old, someone asked me if I wanted to swim across the Golden Gate, a mile swim from San Francisco to Marin, under the Golden Gate Bridge. I had swum numerous one-mile races from the time I was seven, and I enjoyed open water swims, because I felt I could swim as fast as possible for as long as possible without worrying about walls. In this attempt, I could become the youngest girl to swim the Golden Gate while my teammate, Bruce Farley, would try to become the youngest boy to complete the mile swim. We swam for the San Mateo Marlins under the guidance of Ray and Zada Taft. The goal of swimming the Golden Gate was to inspire people of all ages to learn to swim and thus prevent drownings. We marveled at stories of the great marathon swimmers, of the English Channel and other long-distance swims; we even had the privilege of speaking with Gertrude Ederle. We trained for a few months, did a few open water training swims, and at last the date in late September arrived. The swim was to begin at 8 A.M. on September 18, 1965.

Nothing seemed to go well on the morning of the swim. The engine of the main support boat didn't work. Since the tides affect the swim, the timing of the swim was critical. In addition, since this is a major shipping channel, the later the swim began, the more ships we would encounter. While waiting for the boat to be fixed, we were interviewed by the newspaper reporters. A fisherman on the dock began struggling with his line, and after quite a struggle lifted a baby shark onto the dock. The press took pictures of us timidly standing next to the shark until our coaches quickly ushered us away. The shark was as big as I was!

After an hour delay, we left the dock to go to the starting point of the swim off of Fort Point in San Francisco. Since we were late, we decided not to take the time to apply grease; the water was a frigid 56 to 59 degrees F. At 10 years of age, I was 50 inches tall and weighed 50 pounds, compared to Bruce's 85 pounds for the same height. The water was extremely cold. A few minutes into the swim, we had to stop for the first of many ships passing under the Golden Gate Bridge. It was dangerous to get too close to a ship, since we could be pulled under the ship. We just treaded water until the enormous ship passed.

We had planned for a one-mile swim; unfortunately, with the time delay the tides had changed, making the swim close to two miles. With the additional problem of stopping numerous times for ships, the 25- to 30-minute swim was becoming a 45- to 55-minute swim. With less than 400 meters to go, my coach asked if I was cold. I was frozen but swimming well. I responded honestly and was asked if I wanted to get out. She asked me! I said yes and was told to swim to the boat. When I touched the boat, disqualifying myself, I knew I had done something wrong. I climbed on the boat and watched Bruce complete the swim. I cried. I had failed, but I promised myself I would never quit again. Someday I would swim the English Channel. This swim taught me about challenges I had never experienced physically or mentally in the confines of a swimming pool; it inspired me to attempt every open water swim possible.

Open water swimming, whether in a race or part of a triathlon, challenges each swimmer to deal with numerous elements both mentally and physically. Besides these, there are the "unknown" elements—the unanticipated twists of fate. The opportunity to face these obstacles, known and unknown, lures swimmers to the challenge. As you will learn in chapter 2, making sure an open water swim is safe and preparing for anything that could happen are vital for success.

2

Safety in the Water World

S afety is the top priority for swimming. Never train in an unprotected area unless you have someone to train with and you know it is safe. It is better to train in an area with lifeguards, inform them how far you are planning to swim, and give them your basic training schedule. Their knowledge, support, and watchful eyes are always beneficial.

NEVER SWIM ALONE

The first rule of open water swimming is never swim alone. You need to have at least a coach or another swimmer around, or swim in an area protected by a lifeguard to ensure some response if you have a cramp, experience hypothermia, or are attacked by marine life. While these situations rarely occur, it is best to be prepared for any possibility. One ideal way to be sure you never swim alone is to take your coach with you. Having your coach on your training swims can allow you to relax and concentrate on swimming, knowing that your coach can deal with any problems.

Your Coach

An open water swimming coach must be a unique person—willing to work long hours and be very supportive. Look for a coach

of other distance swimmers or a coach of pool swimmers who is willing to work with you full time. However, you may not be able to find anyone with such expertise or time. In reality, your coach need not have an extensive background or experience in training other swimmers or athletes, if you or others around you have enough swimming expertise. You can teach your coach all the intricacies of open water swimming.

Chapter 9 details the coach's responsibilities during a race or individual swim. Here I will explain the coach's general responsibilities. The coach must know you well, your likes and dislikes, and how best to communicate with you. Your coach is responsible for feeding and guiding you, monitoring your stroke rate and stroke efficiency, and ensuring that you are safe from other boats, hazards, marine life, and hypothermia. Performing these responsibilities is vital, whether you are in a race or a practice swim.

A Friend or Family Member

If a coach cannot be with you during open water training swims, have the coach write your workout plan and recruit a friend or family member to be your trainer. A trainer offers important support—a smile, a nudge to get in the water, a companion for a walk on the beach, or support from a boat. This person helps keep you motivated day after day, shares your joy and pain, and is always there for you. It is a tough job, but an essential one. In many cases a good friend, a lover, or a relative can be your biggest asset. You have to work as a team. This person needs to learn how *you* react to cold water, fish, and different people and must know your likes and dislikes, because, in the end, this is the only person besides yourself who can help you during a swim.

During my 1978 English Channel crossing, my mother acted as my trainer. She had never been on a crossing, and at the sixth hour, we were running into the outgoing tide. My mother gave me our prearranged signal to sprint one mile. She continued the signal until I yelled at her to stop. She knew I did not understand why she was asking me to sprint, since I had been going 100 percent for six hours. However, she knew she had to stop me and tell me we were running into an unexpected outgoing tide and that, on previous crossings, the swimmers were aided by an incoming tide.

Since I was hours ahead of the record, I reached this point prior to the tide changing. She knew that I needed to know exactly what was going on, so I could accept it and deal with it. We had spent four months of training, going over every aspect of the swim each day, and this effort paid off. Despite the navigator's warning that this was not a good time to stop, she knew I wanted to know what was going on. In the Channel, a 30-second stop can mean reswimming 400 yards or more. As we hit the outgoing tide, this further complicated the situation, and my mother demanded the stop. I heard what she said and nodded my head. I did not understand why this was happening, since I was experiencing mild hypothermia, but I attempted to give 110 percent. I used every bit of energy I had left. I was able to break through the outgoing tide and reach the French coast at Cape Gris Nez. The decision to sprint paid off. I broke the overall world record by one hour and five minutes.

For triathlons, support crafts or coaches rarely accompany swims. Lifeguards and support crafts patrol the courses to ensure the triathletes' safety. Still, triathletes should have a coach for training and on shore during a race to watch their swim and help them improve in the future.

BE PREPARED FOR ANY SITUATION

The second rule of open water swimming is to be prepared for any type of problem, such as illness, hypothermia, dehydration, marine life, tides, currents, bad weather, or support-craft failure. Expect the unexpected and have a plan of action for each occurrence. As you can see in figure 2.1, open water has many facets. You must prepare for whatever the conditions may bring.

Adapting to Water Temperature

Water temperatures will vary for every swim. In open water races, the water temperature can range from 62 degrees to 78 degrees; for triathlons, the water temperature can range from 56 to 85 degrees, so wet suits are allowed. In individual swims, the water temperature may range from 48 to 90 degrees, but no wet suits are allowed.

Cold water can be extremely difficult to swim in if you are not properly prepared. Any swim in water under 66 degrees will create physiological problems. Table 2.1 lists water temperatures in Fahrenheit and centigrade. The body loses heat more quickly in cold water than in warm water, and dropping body temperature can lead to hypothermia. The physiological changes that warn of approaching hypothermia include the following. First your hands and feet cramp and your face aches. Next, your back cramps; then your hips and legs drop lower in the water. You may be shivering and may have slowed down. Focusing is difficult, so you may have trouble answering questions. Gradually, your upper back will turn blue, then gray, and finally a gray white. At this point, you can no longer answer questions. You *must* be pulled from the water. If you are under 14 or over 50, these physiological changes may occur in water over 66 degrees.

Generally, women have a higher percentage of subcutaneous fat than do men, which assists women in colder water. However, some men have higher body fat than some women; it depends on the individual. Body fat is something an open water swimmer or triathlete can measure while preparing for an open water swim. If a male swimmer has under 8 to 12 percent body fat or a female

Figure 2.1 The ocean can be a tranquil companion . . . but at any moment the tranquility can turn to anger.

TABLE 2.1

Temperature Conversions

Fahrenheit	Centigrade	Fahrenheit	Centigrade
50.0	10	69.8	21
51.8	11	71.6	22
53.6	12	73.4	23
55.4	13	75.2	24
57.2	14	77.0	25
59.0	15	78.8	26
60.8	16	80.6	27
62.6	17	82.4	28
65.4	18	85.2	29
66.2	19	86.0	30
68.0	20		

Note: Fahrenheit = (C × 1.8) + 32; centigrade = (F − 32) × .555.

has under 10 to 16 percent, they can try to gain weight to deal with the cold or try to acclimatize their bodies to cold water. The latter is the best solution.

Adjusting an open water swimmer's body composition used to be thought of as the best method to deal with cold water; most open water swimmers were large and round. Since the 1970s, the trend has been to adapt to water temperature through training instead of gaining weight. Triathletes worry less about body composition, since training for three sports tends to develop a thin but muscular body with a lower percentage of body fat than the open water swimmer might have. As you will learn below, swimmers can adapt using equipment and apparel instead of changing body composition.

The easiest form of protection against cold water is a bathing cap. A cap can prevent as much as 20 percent heat loss from the body. A second aid is a pair of earplugs, which also protect against heat loss from the head. Grease, used to protect the swimmer from chafing, may also help retain body warmth. For triathletes, a wet suit will assist in maintaining warmth. (Wet suits are illegal for open water swims and individual record attempts.)

Prior to entering the water for a workout, stretch and warm up your body by raising your heart rate as well as increasing circulation and lubricating your joints. Chapter 6 discusses some common stretches.

Get into cold water slowly (figure 2.2a). This helps the body adapt. If you dive into the cold water quickly, you may lose your breath, your muscles may tighten so you can't swim, you may go into hypothermia, or you could have a heart attack. Walk into the water. Put your hands in immediately and splash your face (figure 2.2b). Once your hands and face adjust to the temperature, bob up and down, getting your whole body wet. Now swim a few strokes. If you are still too cold, try jogging a little in the water's edge. If this does not work, wait a few minutes and try again. As a last resort, you can urinate in the water. This will warm you for a few minutes, since urine is 98 degrees compared to the colder surrounding temperature of the water. Bob up and down in the warmer water. You can also do this when you are feeding or are stationary in the water during a practice or a swim. Curling your knees under your chin further warms your whole body briefly. Keeping the body warm ensures your muscles and nervous system will work optimally.

When adjusting to the cold water, swim 5 to 20 minutes the first day, and then add anywhere from 5 to 15 minutes a day or

a   b

Figure 2.2 (a) Enter cold water slowly, and (b) dip your hands and splash your face to help your body adapt to the cold.

every other day, depending on the temperature. Let your body be the guide. Cold water is any temperature that you are not comfortable with when you touch the water. If you are tired or hung over, the water will feel colder. If you are cold hours after the practice, do not add time to the next practice until you adjust to the water and warm up faster. This will take longer but is an important adjustment procedure.

Generally, the colder the water, the longer it takes to warm up. In water under 60 degrees, it may take an hour, if you warm up at all. In water 60 to 65 degrees, it may take a half hour, whereas in water 65 to 70 degrees, you may warm up in 10 to 15 minutes. It is important to remember younger and older swimmers or tired swimmers will take longer to warm up.

When I first swam in open water, any temperature under 65 degrees was unbearable. Over the years, I adapted to 50- to 54-degree water. I never enjoyed being cold, but it was necessary to achieve my goal of swimming the English Channel.

As soon as you get out of the water, drink warm fluids, take off your suit, briskly dry your body, and dress warmly. If you are still cold, take a warm shower and drink more warm fluids. A nap may also help.

Guarding Against Hypothermia and Dehydration

Hypothermia is the most dangerous problem facing an open water swimmer. Heat is lost 25 times faster in water than in air at a similar temperature. As the water temperature gets colder, the rate of heat loss increases. In cold water, the blood is vaso-constricted from all the extremities of the body except the head. The temperature at which this occurs varies for each person. However, in any practice or swim under 66 degrees, the coach and/or race officials need to watch for signs of hypothermia. As air temperature drops, you will lose heat through the water and air. If the air temperature is more than 10 degrees colder than the water, you will lose even more heat. Swimming in 70-degree water when the air is 60 degrees may not be a problem. If the water is 60 degrees and the air is 45 degrees, you may have problems unless you have trained in these conditions.

Three Phases of Hypothermia. There are three phases of hypo-thermia: mild, moderate, and severe (see table 2.2). In mild hypothermia, you may have goose bumps and begin to shiver. Your skin will be blue and your body temperature will be be-tween 95 to 98 degrees Fahrenheit. During this phase, warm

TABLE 2.2

Hypothermia		
Phase	**Body temperature**	**Bodily signs**
Mild	95–98 degrees	Conscious, shivering, blue skin
Moderate	90–95 degrees	Conscious, severe shivering, difficulty speaking, trouble answering questions, eyes dilated, gray skin
Severe	85–90 degrees	May be unconscious; grayish white skin; no understanding of questions; trouble recognizing friends; no shivering—rigid

fluids can warm and hydrate your body. Mild hypothermia can be treated with frequent doses of warm fluids during a swim, and you should urinate more often. If you begin to get nervous, your coach should talk calmly to you. If you want to leave the water, do so. Some athletes panic in this stage.

Experiencing mild hypothermia in practice a few times can help you work through the shivering and pain in a race. Once you finish the swim or choose to get out of the water, remove your wet suit as soon as possible. Rub your skin forcefully and put on dry, warm clothes. You may need many layers initially. As you warm up, you will begin to take off the extra layers of warm clothing. Drink warm fluids as soon as possible. If you are still cold, get into a car and turn the heater and fan on high to warm quickly.

In moderate hypothermia, your eyes are dilated, your shivering is more severe, and your skin color is gray. You may refuse liquid or it may spill out the side of your mouth. You will have difficulty speaking and answering questions. A male swimmer may not be able to urinate since the bladder shuts down. Your body temperature drops to 90 to 95 degrees Fahrenheit. Normally, if you are suffering from moderate hypothermia, you will slow your stroke rate and alter the efficiency of your stroke.

If you are almost finished with the swim, that is, within 20 to 30 minutes, you might be able to complete the swim, but emergency personnel should be notified. The coach has to determine if you are in good enough health to finish the swim. If you are over 50 years old, no wondering should occur; you should be taken from the water. Once you have completed the swim or are taken from the water, your movements should be limited and you should not stand or walk for more than a few steps. This precaution is imperative, since your body has shunted the blood from your limbs to protect your heart and brain, the core of your body. The blood in your arms and legs is significantly colder than the blood of the core. If you walk or move too much, this cold blood will circulate to the core, which can cause a heart attack. To prevent this, your support crew should remove the wet suit and warm the core of your body, give you warm fluids, and gradually warm you up (figure 2.3). They should place hot packs over the arteries adjacent to the groin and under each armpit. These actions, plus warm clothes, will help you return to normal temperature. For safety, you should be checked by a doctor.

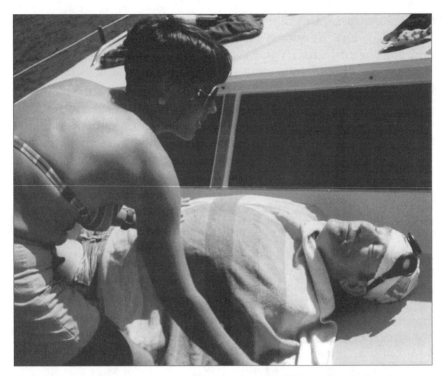

Figure 2.3 Dale Petranech suffering from mild hypothermia after swimming Catalina. He is being warmed and given warm fluids.

Severe hypothermia can result in death. Usually you stop shivering and abruptly become unconscious. Your skin would look grayish white. Your body temperature would be below 90 degrees. You would have to be removed from the water immediately or you might drown. You would need to be taken to a hospital emergency room. Meanwhile, your suit should be removed and you should be placed in a warm sleeping bag or in warm blankets. It is essential that another person get in the bag with you. To help transfer the second person's body heat to you and ultimately increase your chances for survival, this person should be wearing underwear only.

In October of 1977, John York attempted a double crossing of the Catalina Channel from the mainland to the island and back. His goal was to become the first male to swim a double crossing and the first person to swim a double in this direction. The conditions were choppy. On the first leg, John began vomiting. He was seasick. Despite this, he swam well, setting a new men's single crossing world record of 8 hours, 31 minutes, and 20 seconds. He rested three minutes, while he ate some chicken and cookies and drank ERG, a fluid replacement drink. On the return, he continued to vomit. The further he swam, the colder he got. He was experiencing moderate hypothermia. Since his stroke count per minute remained in the high 80s, no one on the boat seemed worried. All of a sudden something went wrong. John became disoriented, and his stroke rate dropped to 66 strokes per minute. He wasn't making any progress, but since he was so close to shore, the support crew encouraged him to finish. John swam eight strokes without breathing. His coach reached over and grabbed him and found him unconscious. His body temperature had dropped to 88 degrees. He had slipped into severe hypothermia. He spent two days in the hospital and nearly died of hypothermia.

In 1978, John returned to the Catalina Channel and conquered it. He shattered his old single crossing record by 50 minutes and shattered the overall double record by almost three hours. He didn't experience any seasickness or hypothermia on this crossing. John went on to swim the English Channel and represent the United States as an open water swimmer and an open water coach for 14 years.

Regardless of the distance of a swim, anyone can become hypothermic. It is imperative for an open water racer or a triathlete to train sufficiently and in similar water temperatures to ensure success without illness.

Dehydration. Dehydration is another medical danger for open water swimmers and triathletes. Dehydration is one of the first symptoms of hypothermia. The early signs include dizziness, fatigue, headache, thirst, loss of appetite, flushed skin, impatience, and weakness. If dehydration continues, you will experience blurred vision, deafness, difficulty swallowing, dry skin, rapid pulse, shortness of breath, lack of saliva, and an inability to stand easily.

To ensure this does not occur, drink eight ounces of fluid every 10 to 15 minutes in training or during a race, if possible. In hot weather or cold water, you may need to drop the time to every 5 to 10 minutes. The support crew also needs to drink fluids. Paddlers and coaches can experience dehydration as easily as a swimmer, which can put you in danger if the support people are at less than 100 percent efficiency. In addition, the support crew should not drink alcohol during your swim since it causes dehydration.

The best types of fluids are cool fluids. Cool fluids are more easily digested. If the water temperature is cold, however, warm the fluids to 85 to 90 degrees. Water is adequate for any swim up to two hours. After two hours, some type of electrolyte fluid is needed (see chapter 9).

Paula Newby-Fraser won the Ironman World Championships seven times. It was considered her race. She is the only woman to have completed the event in under nine hours, setting the course record in 8 hours, 55 minutes, and 28 seconds. Paula owned the Ironman in Kona, at least until October 7, 1995. As she was attempting to win the Ironman for the unbelievable eighth time in a row, disaster struck. While on the bike portion, she threw her food away and stopped eating and drinking. As she approached the finish line of the marathon, she slowed to a walk due to exhaustion and dehydration. She then fell to her knees just 400 meters from the finish. Twenty minutes later, she picked herself up and crossed the finish line, ending the drama in fourth place for the women. In 1996 she returned to Kona and won the race for women.

Paula suffered from dehydration caused by three things. In the 2.4-mile swim, she didn't drink fluid; no one did. During the bike phase, she stopped eating and drinking, and thus she had no energy to replace what she used. For any swim over a half hour, a swimmer needs to drink fluids, especially if the athlete is a triathlete and has two more stages of the competition. Fluids will be discussed further in chapter 9.

Not only can dehydration stop even the greatest Ironman competitor for women, it can even kill. Taking in fluids and food is vital for the muscles and body to perform and therefore is vital for success. Plan your drinking and feeding during practice, and follow your plan during a race as a top priority. This may make the difference between success and failure.

Protecting Yourself From Sunburn

In addition to hydrating the body, be sure to put sunscreen on your neck and back as well as your arms and legs. Apply sunscreen at least 30 minutes before a swim practice or race. Use a fair amount and make sure to rub it into the skin. A strong sun block of at least a 30 sun protection factor (SPF) rating is best. It is important to use a product that protects the skin from both UVA and UVB rays, and an SPF of 30 blocks out 96.67 percent of both rays. Choose a sunscreen that also stays on at least six hours in the water. Some of the brands on the market that fit these criteria are Alligator, Bullfrog, Coppertone Sport, and Arena Sport. The support crew also needs to wear sunscreen.

The support crew should wear strong sunglasses that block the sun's rays and water glare. The glasses should have UVA, UVB, and UVC protection. Some of my favorite brands are Fila, Gargoyles, Oakley, Ray-Ban, Revo, Sungear, and Vuarnet. These range in price from $40 to $130 (US).

Protecting Against Ear Infection

Another problem which swimmers need to protect against is an ear infection. Whether you are swimming in a lake, river, ocean, or pool, an ear infection is possible. After each swim, put an ear solution into your ears. This can be a pharmacy's prescription of 70 percent alcohol with 2 percent salicylic acid or an over-the-counter brand.

OBSERVE YOUR SURROUNDINGS

Prior to entering the water, it is very important to survey the beach, lake front, or river where you plan to train. As you walk the beach, observe how the shoreline changes. Look for landmarks on the shore, such as telephone poles, buildings, homes, and lifeguard towers. Not only can you use these as distance markers, but as safety markers as well. The water itself is another important area to survey. Check for buoys, ropes, old pilings, or drains that may be detrimental to you during low tide. These may be hidden in high tide.

Differences Among River, Lake, and Ocean Swimming

It is vital to your safety to learn to appreciate and respect where you train, whether it be a lake, river, or ocean. There are differences among river, lake, and ocean swimming that swimmers must take into account. In most cases, a river has some type of current or assistance. The center of the current's flow is where the water moves the fastest. The water in the current's center is choppy, which may be uncomfortable to you. Near the shore, the water is still. Some rivers have back-moving eddies at the shore. A back-eddy is water circulating opposite the flow of the river, and the water is moving backwards. An eddy can be identified by a line of water where the flow of the river and the back-eddy meet.

A lake may also have a current flow, which is caused by rivers entering or leaving the lake. If the lake is in a windy area, the wind will affect the movement of water. The wind will move the top layer of the water, creating choppy conditions. One further distinction of a fresh water lake (or a river) over the ocean is temperature. A 60-degree lake will feel similar to the ocean at 55 degrees. The lake is a more intense cold. This 5-degree difference is significant and must be taken into account for a lake or river swim. This difference in how you experience temperatures seems to have something to do with the properties of fresh and salt water. While there have been no tests to substantiate this assertion, any swimmer who has swum in fresh and salt water will verify that swimming in fresh water feels significantly colder than swimming in salt water at the same temperature.

Consider the type of water when training in different mediums. For example, in 1986 and in 1990, there were two good U.S. marathon swimmers who swam well in the ocean but didn't do

well in lakes. In both instances, the ocean and lake swims were the same temperature. In the ocean, neither experienced hypothermia, but both did in the lake, and one had to be pulled from an international race.

A final distinction is that tides, currents, and winds all affect an ocean swim. It is normal to have one- to eight-foot waves at the beginning or end of an ocean swim. A wave is measured by total height from the crest to the trough. Thus, for an eight-foot wave, four feet are above and four are below the still water level. When you are in the trough of the wave, below the still water level and looking upward, the wave always looks huge compared to being on the crest or standing on the shore. This is important to remember when swimming in or out from the shore, because many swimmers get nervous about big waves; some even panic and are hit by the wave, tossing them to the bottom.

Tides have the biggest effect on the ocean and thus on ocean swimming. In England, for example, this flow difference is between 4 and 12 feet from low to high tide. The moon, the sun, and the gravitational forces of the earth control tidal movement. Specific tidal charts are made a year in advance, listing the low tide and high tide times and the size differences between the two. The flow difference reflects how far the water moves up the beach from low to high tide and thus how much water is moving during this time.

There are two types of tides, spring and neap. A *spring tide* has the greatest amount of water movement. This means it also has the strongest flow. A *neap tide* has a small amount of water movement and therefore the least forceful flow. Most channel swims are attempted during neap tides, since it is easier to swim in water which is not changing significantly from low to high tide. If you don't consider the type of tide and flow difference, you may attempt to swim against a strong tide with a large flow difference, which is not possible for most swimmers (if any at all) to overcome. A storm can also make the tidal changes more severe and usually creates larger waves, even if the storm is thousands of miles away.

I was training in France for my English Channel swim in the month of May; the water was 50 degrees F. I didn't check the low and high tides on the first day, since this had not been of concern in my training in California. On this first day, I had planned to swim 30 minutes. The tide was in, but as I swam, it quickly receded. When I finished, I was 100 yards from the shore. I was extremely cold, with gnarled hands, and I could barely walk. It took me over six hours to warm up that day. From that day I learned to check tide charts (figure 2.4).

Undertows and Riptides

You may experience undertows and riptides in the ocean. The undertow follows the wave's break as the water is pulled toward the next wave. If you are caught in the undertow, know that it only lasts until the next wave arrives. Take a breath before the next wave reaches you and try to swim in with the next wave. A riptide is created in areas of multiple waves and limited sand, where the water moves quickly away from the shore. The riptide can be spotted from the shore, since the water is a different color and appears to be choppier than the surrounding water. If you happen to swim into a riptide, swim diagonally across the current, angling toward the shore. Do not swim directly toward shore. If it is too strong, relax and let the water push you. Once

Figure 2.4 Low tide at Folkestone Beach, England reveals a long walk to shore for any swimmer who miscalculates.

you relax and feel a lesser pull, swim parallel to shore for 200 to 400 yards; then swim into the beach. Many times the riptide is fairly narrow. Just remember to stay calm.

In the ocean, it is normal to experience one- to three-foot waves. It is rare to swim in the ocean without some waves. So plan for waves in practice and expect them in a race or individual crossing.

Marine Life

In over 20 years of open water swimming, I have seen only two sharks, a few sting rays, and numerous jellyfish, all during training swims. In a race, the noise and splashing of the other swimmers frighten any marine life away, as do the engines of support craft in individual swims. There are three types of ocean life you should be especially aware of when swimming: seaweed, jellyfish, and sharks. In lakes and in some slow-moving areas of a river, you need to be concerned with reeds and leeches.

Seaweed. Seaweed is a marine plant which floats on or near the surface. Swimming into seaweed can cause you to panic and start thrashing as it wraps itself around you. It is best to remain calm and swim easily through the slimy plants. At times, the plants may be so thick you are literally climbing over them. Slowly lift your arms out of the seaweed and pull yourself across the top of the plants. Try not to kick, since kicking tends to wrap the weed around your legs. Do your best to float high in the water and slide across the surface.

Jellyfish. Jellyfish like to float near the surface of the water on sunny days. Their colors range from transparent to purple and white, which makes them very difficult to spot in the water. If you can avoid them by rolling out of the way, do so. Jellyfish have tentacles that possess a poison and can leave a sting and a subsequent welt on your body. These stings and welts burn, and there is little you can do in training or a swim to alleviate the pain (although a good scream at the time may help). Later, wash the area thoroughly with vinegar or rubbing alcohol. Aspirin will relieve the pain. If you swell severely, see a doctor immediately, since you are probably having an allergic reaction to the sting.

In many instances, if there are only a few jellyfish, you can roll out of the way or adjust your stroke so you don't hit one. Jellyfish were prevalent in the 1970s but seem to have declined since then, at least in the waters around the United States. Portuguese man-of-wars are a larger type of jellyfish, and the aptain Mathew Webb was the first person to swim the English Channel. He accomplished this feat on August 23, 1875 on his second attempt, with a time of 21 hours and 40 minutes, swimming from England to France. Not only was the swim significant as the first successful swim, but his course was altered by the tides, making the ordinarily 20-mile swim considerably longer.

As figure 2.5 demonstrates, Webb was pushed west, then east, followed by another larger western push, and finally by a huge eastern push, ending with a landing in Calais. Most English Channel swimmers follow a variation of this crossing. Missing the coast is the largest single reason for a swimmer to quit the attempt to conquer the Channel. For most swimmers, the thought of swimming another six hours while waiting for the tide to change is too demoralizing, painful, and cold to endure. This is one reason why only just over 800 of over 4,370 attempts have been successful since the formation of the Channel Swimming Association in 1927.

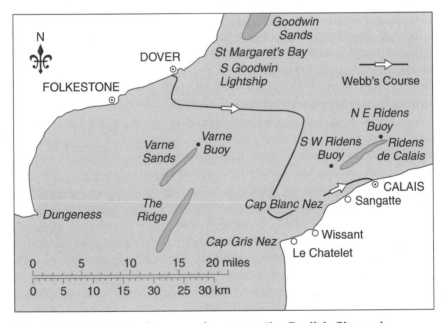

Figure 2.5 Webb's pioneer swim across the English Channel.

stings are more severe. The man-of-war stings are only deadly, however, if you are allergic to them.

Sharks. Sharks are the first thing anyone will ask you about when you tell them you are an open water swimmer. But your chances of being attacked are minimal, especially if you swim in protected areas. For a solo swim, the navigator should have a person aboard trained to deal with sharks. The navigator should have a bang stick and a rifle aboard. Let the navigator worry about such things—you just swim.

In a mass swim, the event coordinator should have a plan to deal with sharks if they appear in the racecourse. Normally, just revving a boat's engine will scare a shark away. To my knowledge there has not been a shark attack in any major Channel swim or ocean race for swimmers or triathletes. This knowledge may not relieve fear of the unknown or the reporter's interest in a shark story, but it can relieve fear of sharks.

In 1976 I made the mistake of watching *Jaws* when it came to the theater. For the next week in practice, on a daily basis, I heard the soundtrack of the shark preparing for an attack. I never saw a shark, but I was scared for the whole week. Finally I used the soundtrack as a signal to speed up. It became a joke. After I swam Catalina, a reporter asked me if I was worried about sharks. Jokingly, I responded that I was scared only when I heard the soundtrack from Jaws; he thought I was serious and detailed this in his article on the swim. Fear of the unknown and/or marine life can be enormous, but gradually you can conquer this fear as you gain experience training in open water.

Fish. You may encounter other fish in lakes, rivers, and oceans. These may swim close to you and may even touch you. In many cases, you can feel the panic of the fish as it scurries off, but this doesn't stop your heart rate from climbing as you panic briefly. Some fish may nibble at your foot but usually won't bite. To put this into perspective, think of the size of a one- to two-foot fish compared to a five- or six-foot swimmer (figure 2.6). The fish doesn't know the swimmer isn't a huge predator! This thought always made me laugh after my heartbeat raced for a few seconds due to a brush with a fish.

Lake Reeds. In a lake, reeds can limit your ability to cross the area. Most races start and finish in a clear area. If you find yourself swimming in reeds, progress slowly and remain calm. Look for the easiest escape route, even if it means backtracking a small amount; this will save you time over slogging through the reeds.

Leeches. Leeches are nasty-looking creatures which may attach themselves to you in the water. However, leeches are rarely encountered, and if they are, their bite is relatively painless. (Leeches were used medicinally for bloodletting for centuries, since it was a painless treatment.) The best way to detach a leech is to light a match and burn it off. Apply hydrogen peroxide as soon as possible to the wound; clean it a second time with hydrogen peroxide, and then use soap and water. There may be some bleeding where the leech attached itself, but it will not hurt. The worse part is often the fear of the leech attaching to you rather than the actual occurrence.

Figure 2.6 Huge fish caught while the United States National Open Water Swim Team trained in a lake in Wisconsin.

WATCH THE WEATHER

Numerous weather conditions can affect a swim. Fog is dangerous, since you can lose sight of the shore and not know which way to go. If you are alone at the ocean and decide to enter in fog, swim parallel to shore. Do not go out past the wave line. If there are piers or other natural landmarks, try to swim within these landmarks. Usually the waves are smaller when there is dense fog. If you go out too far, you could get lost. Stop, listen for waves breaking, start calling for help, and do not move. Hopefully, the fog will clear or you will figure out where you are. The best solution is to wait until the fog disappears before entering the water.

Electric storms can also pose dangerous situations. If you are swimming in a lake, river, or ocean and a storm begins, leave the water immediately. If you live in an area which has lots of electric storms, check the weather conditions before entering the water. If there are afternoon thunderstorms most of the summer, try to train early in the morning. To determine if the lightning is dangerous, once you see the lightning, count the seconds until you hear the thunder. A five-second delay between the lightning and the thunder means the storm is only one mile away. In most cases, when a storm is five miles away or closer, you should leave the water. Remember that lightning can travel horizontally for five miles. Lightning is also a danger to support crafts, since the craft is higher in the water than the swimmer. Safety is most important; you have to work around Mother Nature.

Hurricanes and severe rainstorms should keep you from the water. Many of these storms create huge waves, making it very challenging to swim on the surface. Most of the time, you will be diving under the waves, sneaking a breath, and then diving back under the waves. Twenty minutes of this can be exhausting. In addition, in many places when the storm drains are full, the water overflows into the river, lake, or ocean, carrying with it all sorts of garbage and even sewage. Therefore, this is not a healthy time or place to swim.

You may prefer to swim at night, since there is less boat traffic and the waters are usually calmer. The navigator will decide what time an individual swim will begin and whether it will be a day or night swim. In the Catalina Channel, it is better to swim at night, since there are fewer noncommercial boats in the channel and the wind tends to calm down in the late evening hours. In the English Channel, there are so many commercial vessels at all hours of the day and night that the Coast Guard prefers that swimmers not swim at night.

In 1989, the U.S. Swimming (USS) national open water swimming team decided to swim a relay across the Catalina Channel. The goal was to break the world record of eight and a half hours. The team consisted of Jay Wilkerson, Chad Hundeby, Jim McConica, Karen Burton, Martha Jahn, and Erika Reetz. The swim was to begin just after midnight to take advantage of the calmer ocean and less boat traffic. Each athlete would swim a one-hour leg. After six hours, the swimmers would continue in the same order until the team reached Catalina. The tactic was to set the order with the fastest swimmer going first and ending with the slowest. As stated earlier, a problem emerged when this was discussed with the swimmers. Chad Hundeby was the fastest swimmer, but he did not want to swim in the dark, so he was rescheduled for a daylight leg. This was not the best order for breaking a record but was necessary in order to deal with Chad's fears. The crossing went well and the team set a new record of seven hours and two minutes which still stands today.

In the next few years, Chad overcame his fear of darkness and sharks. In 1994 he swam a solo crossing of the Catalina Channel, leaving at 12:22 A.M. He set a new world record of 8 hours, 14 minutes, and 46 seconds. As this story demonstrates, sometimes athletes should not be pushed. Rather, they may need assistance to deal with their fears and hopefully conquer them, as Chad did.

To ensure a safe open water experience, you need to be aware of the preceding factors and have a plan of action for any emergency which may crop up. If you do practice swims in safe, protected areas, you should be fine. For more difficult swims or rougher conditions, you should have a support craft with you. By taking the above precautions, and properly equipping yourself and your support craft as detailed in the next chapter, your training and races should be successful.

3

Equipment for the Open Water

Accorording to national and international open water rules, swimming equipment includes a suit, cap, and goggles. For triathletes, wet suits are also legal. Find the brand and equipment that fit you best and most comfortably. Also, determine which type of support craft, if allowable, is best for your different swims or races.

SWIMSUITS

Many swimsuits on the market are suitable for open water swimming. The only rule regarding swimsuits, according to both United States Swimming (USS) and the Federation Internationale de Natation Amateur (FINA), is that the suit can't aid in buoyancy or warmth. The most comfortable swimsuit is a suit made with lycra and nylon. It is a soft suit that conforms to the body. The nylon suit is the most durable; however, it lacks flexibility and, with continued use of petroleum jelly on the straps, the suit will become stiff and uncomfortable.

Women have the further option of a one-piece or two-piece suit (both are legal according to USS and FINA rules). In warmer water, many athletes prefer a two-piece suit, since there is less suit so the body stays cooler. Again, this is an individual choice.

One specific feature that a woman swimmer should assess when deciding on a swimsuit is the width of the strap. A thinner strap can reduce chafing. A thick strap may mean more chafing. If you are swimming in salt water, this difference can be significant. A chafing rub can take months to heal, because the sore will reopen every day you train. Also, the salt will make the cut worse and more painful each day. Only time away from the water will help a chafing sore heal.

The six major suit companies are Speedo, Arena, Hind, Tyr, Nike, and Water Wear. Each has different hip and leg cuts, back styles, straps, and overall styles and patterns for a women's suit and variations of hip and leg cuts for a men's suit (figure 3.1). A suit will range in cost from $15 to $30 (US) for a men's suit and $30 to $75 (US) for a women's suit. Experiment with each suit before you use it in a major competition or swim. Comfort and ease of movement should be your primary concern.

Courtesy of Speedo

Figure 3.1 Swimsuits allow easy movement, and body suits (described next) provide added warmth. The choice is yours.

BODY SUITS

A body suit differs from a regular swimsuit in that a body suit covers more of the body. Water Wear makes the only body suit on the market and offers it in three designs: full body, covering arms and legs; hip covering with half the arms covered; and hip covering with sleeveless arms. The more body the suit covers, the more warmth it provides. These suits are legal in all races and international swims. However, they may have more spots for chafing, since each covers more of the body than a normal suit. Practicing with the suit will reveal any problem areas, and you can protect these with petroleum jelly. You will have to experiment with these suits in both fresh and salt water. Ultimately, your decision will be based on personal preference.

WET SUITS

Wet suits are legal for triathlons and some masters races but illegal for most USS-sanctioned swims, channel swims, and international competitions. The reason for this rule is that the challenge of the swim is to match the swimmer against the elements. Wet suits help a swimmer stay warm and aid in buoyancy. This extra help may enable swimmers to complete swims they may otherwise have had to quit. Also, the extra lining under the chest helps the swimmer float higher in the water. This alters the swimmer's body position and lifts the legs. This improved positioning reduces drag and, therefore, increases the swimmer's speed. The extra buoyancy will help a slower swimmer or a swimmer with bad form to swim faster, from two to four minutes a mile. This is a great advantage for any swimmer.

Most long distance swimmers and the faster triathletes consider the use of a wet suit as an unfair advantage and consider the swimmer or triathlete who wears one to be less tough. Many thinner long distance swimmers, however, are in favor of wet suits to help them keep warm and thus complete more races. From a purely safety standpoint, the wet suit should be allowed in colder swims under 60 degrees and for older swimmers.

As long as wet suits are legal, many triathletes will use them to swim faster. Triathletes will not use a wet suit if the water is warm and a wet suit may cause overheating, or in a short race to save a few seconds in the changeover.

Two types of materials are used for wet suits: polyolefin and neoprene. Polyolefin is heavier than lycra but lighter than neoprene. Since polyolefin has some insulating ability, it is classified as a wet suit. However, this suit doesn't get as heavy as a neoprene wet suit when wet. You can purchase any of these suits from Aeroskin for anywhere from $25 to $115 (US).

Neoprene wet suits come in short and full. The short suit is sleeveless and comes with or without a hood. It covers the legs only to the middle of the thighs. This suit is best when the water is not too cold or the distance is short. The short wet suit helps with buoyancy as well as warmth. Short wet suits are sold by DK Douglas, O'Neill, Promotion, and Quintana Roo and cost between $35 and $129 (US).

Full wet suits, which cover the legs to the ankles, are manufactured in two variations. One is sleeveless and the other has sleeves to the wrist (figure 3.2, *a* and *b*). If your arms don't tend

Courtesy of ProMotion

a   *b*

Figure 3.2 ProMotion's (*a*) short sleeve wet suit and (*b*) long sleeve wet suit.

to get cold, you may want to buy a sleeveless wet suit, since it will allow you to feel the water and thus help you keep proper mechanics within your stroke. If you are swimming in cold water, your arms may get very cold, and you won't be able to feel your stroke at all. In this case, the long-sleeve model is the best choice. Full wet suits are made by Henderson, Ironman, O'Neill, Promotion, and Quintana Roo. The cost ranges from $150 to $350 (US).

The conditions and your background will dictate which suit to use. Wear the suit in practice to discover rub areas and to check comfort. It may take you some time to acclimate to a suit, so the sooner you use it, the better.

Find a wet suit that fits your height, body build, and sex. A unisex wet suit may be too loose or too tight in different places. Decide if you want a collar or not. Do you want a suit with a pull cord? The pull cord makes it easier to remove the wet suit quickly. Do you want feel of the water, warmth, or buoyancy? Can you have all of these? Which type is easier to swim in? Is there a difference in warmth between the different wet suits? You need to answer these questions before settling on a suit. Many companies offer a 14-day trial. Take advantage of this opportunity and try a few of them. Be sure to wear each in the cold water. This trial could save you money, cold swims, and pain in the future.

GOGGLES

Goggles are probably the most important piece of equipment you will purchase. Each individual's facial bone structure is different. Therefore, you need to find the pair of goggles that best fits your face, remains watertight, and is comfortable to you (figure 3.3). This choice can be difficult. There are over 100 different styles on the market. Also, if you have eye problems, you can have special goggles made to fit your prescription. A pair of goggles ranges in cost from $4 to $30 (US); a prescription pair is closer to $100 (US).

The following anecdote demonstrates the importance of goggles: In my 1976 crossing of the Catalina Channel, I finished the record-setting swim with my right eye swollen shut. As I swam through the waves at the beginning of the swim, a fish went down my suit. I pulled it out and unfortunately got petroleum jelly on my hand. When I quickly checked my goggles, I put the petroleum jelly on the lining of the goggles. The goggles leaked

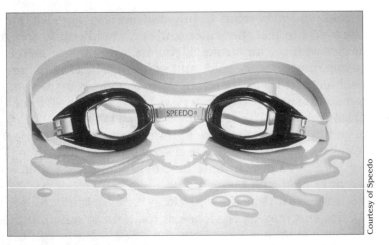

Courtesy of Speedo

Figure 3.3 Goggles come in many styles and colors. Find the ones that best fit your face and your needs.

on one side, and the salt caused my eye to swell. I couldn't see the boat or paddler on my right side for the whole swim; this made me feel confused and disoriented—plus, it was painful! I should have switched pairs but didn't want to stop, even for a short time.

Besides style, goggles come in different colors. The clear lens is helpful at night and in the early morning. The dark lens is good on sunny days. A blue lens is beneficial in fog. Again, personal preference can determine which color of goggles is best for you. Once you find a pair of goggles you like, adjust the nose piece and strap to fit your head; be sure to cut off any extra nose piece or strap. Using an antifog liquid, which can be purchased at an eyewear store, will help keep the lens clear.

SWIM CAPS

The cap is a necessary item for open water swimming safety and body warmth. The brighter the cap, the better, since it will protect you from being run over by a windsurfer or a small boat and will help a lifeguard or trainer keep an eye on you. Again, there are many types of caps, and you should experiment to find which cap feels the most comfortable (figure 3.4). The main types are latex and lycra. Latex doesn't absorb water but may make you too hot in warm water. Lycra absorbs water but may keep your head cooler in warmer water.

Courtesy of Speedo

Figure 3.4 Latex caps come in a rainbow of colors.

Under USS and FINA rules, the cap can't be made of a material which assists in warmth. This means neoprene caps are illegal; however, for many of the masters races and triathlons, this type of cap is legal. Since 20 percent of body heat is lost through the head, a neoprene cap is beneficial when it is legal, especially for older swimmers and for swims in colder water.

EARPLUGS

If you have a tendency to get cold or you spend a significant amount of time in cold water, consider wearing earplugs. These are legal, according to USS, FINA, masters, and triathlon rules. Speedo makes two types which are very good. Both can be adjusted to the shape of your ear. Also, you want earplugs that prevent the water from entering your inner ear. Earplugs reduce heat loss from your head and keep cold water from reaching your inner ear and affecting your balance.

GREASE

To avoid chafing and heat loss, you can use a form of grease. Grease is legal for all national and international races as long as it is not considered excessive, which is determined by the race or individual swim referee. In 20 years of coaching, I have never seen a referee challenge the amount of grease on a swimmer.

Figure 3.5 United States team greased and prepared for the start in Windermere.

Depending on the water temperature, you may only need to grease the core of your body; in water under 58 degrees F, you may want to cover your arms and legs as well (figure 3.5).

There are two types of grease—petroleum jelly and lanolin. Petroleum jelly tends to wear off fairly easily, whereas lanolin does not. Lanolin feels like a thin coating on your body. However, studies on lanolin have demonstrated that it does not help keep you warm. In fact, some swimmers feel that any grease tends to keep the cold in more than the warmth. However, if one is standing on a boat or on the shore and lanolin is applied it feels as if there is a windbreaker on the body. It has been shown that lanolin tends to block the skin pores, which is very dangerous for older swimmers. Therefore, it is not a good idea for older open water swimmers or triathletes to use lanolin. Another option is to carefully heat the lanolin and add Vaseline. Experiment with each of these types of grease and use whatever is most helpful, if anything at all.

Always apply grease with rubber gloves; otherwise, it will stay on your hands. There is a good chance that this grease will get on your goggles and cause numerous problems. In addition, it is important to clean up after applying the grease, so it doesn't spill on the boat.

In 1950, Florence Chadwick broke Gertrude Ederle's record (which had stood for 24 years) for swimming the English Channel. In 1952, she attempted to swim the Catalina Channel, but she had to quit a mile from shore; she was too cold. It was estimated 15 to 20 thousand people were waiting for her to finish. However, she trained for six weeks and tried again, this time wearing 10 pounds of grease. She was just as cold, but was able to fight through the pain and finish.

GUARDING AGAINST CHAFING

Chafing is a nasty element of open water swimming. It occurs anywhere on the body where skin rubs against skin or the suit rubs against skin. For women, normal problem areas are the underarms, on the sides of the neck due to the suit straps, and the back of the neck if a cap is worn. Problem areas for men are the groin area, face, and neck. For men, facial hair growing back from shaving can be disastrous. You must shave on the morning of a swim. The alternative is to let your beard grow to avoid sharp stubble. These sharp hairs rub on the shoulder and neck and can cause deep cuts. For both men and women, dabbing a little petroleum jelly on the problem areas prior to each workout or a race should help prevent chafing. With the salt of the ocean, chafing marks can easily become cuts. Cuts are very difficult to get rid of without leaving the water; therefore, prevention is a must.

EQUIPMENT FOR RACE DAY

Place all of your equipment for race day in one bag and label it "swimmer's equipment." Mark each extra pair of goggles, set of earplugs, cap, and suit in the order to be used. Also, label your food and keep it with your equipment for easy access during a race. Race day preparation is discussed in more detail in chapter 9. Below are lists of equipment you need for practice and each type of swim.

Equipment list for practice, short race, or triathlon

1 suit

2 pairs of goggles

2 caps

1 set of earplugs (if cold water)

1 container of petroleum jelly

1 wet suit (if legal)

a towel

warm clothes (if swim only)

a swim bag with emergency information—name and number of doctor, contact information for family members, and medical insurance information

Equipment list for a marathon swim

2 suits—tested

3 caps—tested and marked

3 pairs of goggles—tested and marked

2 towels

1 set of earplugs—tested and marked

1 to 4 containers of petroleum jelly or lanolin, gloves, small towel, plastic bag

1 wet suit (if legal)

1 pair of shorts

2 T-shirts

1 pair of sweats

street clothes

1 warm coat

ice chest with food for swim

swim bag for swim equipment

emergency information—name and number of doctor, contact information for family members, and medical insurance information

Being prepared with extra suits, caps, goggles, and earplugs can assist in a successful training swim or race. Preparing for cold or injury can alleviate problems. Having proper equipment keeps your focus on the swim, not on your equipment. Taking the time to test and retest your spare equipment will save you time, energy, and frustration on race day. Careful preparation is a key to a successful swim and reaching your goals.

SUPPORT CRAFT

Many types of craft are available for open water swimming. These range from the simple paddleboard to 20- to 100-foot support vessels, and depending on the length of the swim or the conditions, a support craft may be needed. In a race under 11 miles, only a paddleboard, canoe, or kayak may be needed. If the water is cold or you are under 14 or over 50 years old, a larger support craft may be needed. For any individual swim, a larger craft will be needed, since a coach and an official observer must be near you at all times. You must plan for a support craft if it is allowed and you want one.

Paddleboard

The paddleboard is the simplest of the crafts. It is similar to a surfboard but longer and thinner. The paddler can either lie face down and paddle with two hands in unison or sit on the board and use a shorter two-arm stroke (figure 3.6). This craft allows a coach or the support person to be right next to you, which makes feeding and communication ideal. One of the negatives of this craft is that it can be taxing on the paddler. A coach may not be able to paddle, so someone else needs to be trained as a coach. It is also difficult for the paddler to carry much food on the board; therefore, it is either carried on the paddler's back or attached to the board with bungee cords. In choppy seas, it is difficult to get the board through the waves while keeping the gear on the board and maintaining balance, all while trying to feed you.

To feed you, the paddler has to stop to get the food while you proceed unprotected or unguided for a short period. After a quick feeding, you can proceed immediately while the paddler puts things away. (Again, you are unescorted for this short period of time.) If the paddler already had trouble keeping up with you, the paddler may never be able to make up this short distance, and you and the paddler will be stranded. Unfortunately, this

Figure 3.6 Swimmer guided by paddlers in the Catalina Channel.

happens to someone in every open water swim. To avoid this problem, train with a paddler before a swim to ensure that the paddler can keep pace with you and understands the paddler's duties.

Losing a paddler happens quite often. Karen Burton's paddler fell behind at the 16-mile Seal Beach race in 1989. Since Karen was close enough to the male leaders, she was able to guide off of the lead boat. When she needed fluid, a small craft quickly delivered it and then disappeared. This wasn't ideal or safe, but she was able to win the race without a paddler.

Canoe

Another type of craft is a one- or two-person canoe (figure 3.7). This craft can be better than the paddleboard because gear can be stowed on the bottom of the craft instead of on the paddler's back and it is easier to control than a paddleboard. The paddlers can switch position, allowing a fatigued paddler to rest or prepare a feeding, while the other keeps the canoe with you. The

Figure 3.7 Swimmer guided by a canoe in a lake.

negatives include the possibility of hitting you with the paddle if you or the canoe veers off course and the possibility of swamping or dumping the canoe in rough weather.

Kayak

A third type of craft is the sit-on-top closed sea kayak, which can be used in an ocean, lake, or river swim (figure 3.8). A kayak

Figure 3.8 Swimmer guided by a kayak in the Catalina Channel.

is paddled by one person and allows the paddler to sit with a comfortable back support. This is a much easier paddle than a board or a canoe. The sea kayak also stores gear easily, and if extra gear is needed, it can be attached to the bow. The paddler can watch your stroke easily from a kayak. If the kayak tips over, an experienced kayaker can easily right it. This craft allows for easy feeding and close communication, and if an unconscious person rescue is needed, it can be easily accomplished with the sea kayak. More and more open water swimmers are moving to this type of support craft.

Rowboat

The two-person rowboat allows for close communication and ease of carrying gear. It can be close to you in the water but can be dangerous if you or the boat veers off course. This is a reasonably good craft in fair weather but can fill with water in a storm. If the rowers are not in shape, they may have trouble keeping up with a fast swimmer.

Small Powerboat

A small powerboat, with a five- to seven-and-a-half-horsepower engine, can serve as an ideal support craft for all types of open water venues. If the boat has a big engine, a fitting can be placed on the engine to allow it to motor at a slow speed. This boat can carry gear and remain close to you without all the work of a rowboat. The danger lies in the chance that the wind, current, or navigation could move the boat into you or push you into the engine blades. You and the boat driver must constantly watch for these dangers. During a long swim, the driver will fatigue as you get tired, and one mistake by either could create an accident. On a small boat, a coach usually accompanies you, and it is part of the coach's job to ensure that the driver steers clear of you. When you break for feeding or communication, the driver must put the engine into neutral for safety.

In rough weather, this boat may take on water, creating numerous problems, such as difficulty in steering or the possibility of sinking of the boat. There is an option for a small boat and rough conditions—use a sea anchor, which looks like a small parachute and trails off the back of the boat. The sea anchor allows for better control of the boat and thus easier navigation. A sea anchor was used in the USS 16-mile nationals in 1994; there were six-foot waves, and many of the boats were being knocked all over the course. The boat accompanying Chad Hundeby had a sea anchor, and the driver was able to control the boat. This saved Chad from swimming extra miles and from much frustration during the swim.

The other negative of this small craft is that it emits fumes. If the wind blows the fumes into you, they could make you sick. The navigator needs to keep the boat downwind of you and adjust the boat's position when the wind changes.

Large Craft

On long swims of over 10 miles or dangerous solo swims, a boat of 30 to 70 feet is usually used. On certain crossings, no other crafts are allowed in the water. You must watch the boat and adjust your course with the boat. In rough weather, this can be difficult. If other craft are legal, paddleboards or kayaks can be used as extra support close to you. The large boat allows for a coach, numerous support people, and extra paddlers to be on board, ensuring there are enough support people in case of an emergency. The negatives of this large craft are trying to keep the boat at the slow pace of the swimmer, diesel fumes emitted from the boat, and switching paddlers in and out of the water. Again, the sea anchor can be used for better navigation and slower speeds. The navigator also needs to keep the boat downwind of you, as is recommended above with the small craft.

ESSENTIAL ON-BOAT EQUIPMENT

Regardless of which craft you use, you need certain essential pieces of equipment.

Radio

The radio is a vital piece of equipment. If you are in trouble, your coach can call for help. For most mass races, there is a radio channel for the race. The crew can also use the radio to get information on your position and that of other competitors in the race. In addition, your crew can keep in contact with someone on shore who can keep family and friends informed of the swim. If the coach is working with more than one athlete in a race, the coach may keep in contact with each via the radio. To use the radio, each country requires permits. Obtaining a permit is a simple process of filling out a form and can forestall fines or protests from race officials.

This use of a radio was first introduced in 1990 at the World Cup in Lake Windermere, England. Members of the U.S. team were able to communicate with each other throughout the race with radios. If a swimmer from another team tried to make a move, this information was relayed to the other coaches quickly. This helped the U.S. team finish first overall, setting both the men's and women's records on the course.

Navigational Resources

The final two pieces of equipment necessary are either a compass or a navigational computer and a chart of the swim course. Whether you are using a small craft or a large one, a compass and chart are necessary items. Swimming the shortest distance is the goal. The navigational computers and compass will be discussed in greater detail in chapter 4.

Below is a suggested list of other equipment to have on board a support craft:

- Marker board and pens
- Notebook with pencil and pens
- Stopwatch or watch with second hand
- Thermos bottles filled with swimmer's choice of fluid
- Plastic cups for feeding
- Radio
- Four hot packs
- First aid kit
- Seasick medicine
- Six light sticks
- Compass or navigational computer device
- Chart of swim course

If you are using a larger craft (30 to 70 feet), then include the following additional equipment:

- Three waterproof flashlights and extra batteries (if a night swim) or equivalent
- Duct tape (if a night swim) or four stretch cords

- Two paddleboards or kayaks
- Extra thermos bottles
- Five squirt bottles
- Two additional hot water bottles
- Old blankets or sleeping bag to protect from cold
- Camera, film, flash
- Seasick pills
- Five wet suits for paddlers
- Five white T-shirts for night paddling
- Peterson lifeguard tube
- Important emergency and press telephone numbers
- Pole with net [to pick up fluid bottle or something dropped off side of boat]

Once you decide to use a support craft, you need to understand basic navigation. You will learn about navigation in chapter 4.

4

The Shortest Distance Between Start and Finish

Navigation is, quite simply, getting from where you are to where you want to go. This statement may seem obvious, but it points out the two fundamental things you need to know if you are going to efficiently navigate from point A to point B. You need to know where you are and where you want to go. Amazingly enough, open water swimmers and their support crew frequently don't know exactly where they are during a swim. It is a necessity for open water swimming and the swim leg of triathlons to take navigation into account in order to swim the best race possible, that is, the shortest and smartest distance. This chapter focuses on the best ways to effectively and safely navigate for an open water swim, whether it be a triathlon swim leg using line-of-sight navigation, the Seal Beach 10-mile with a kayaker accompanying the swimmer, or swimming the English Channel with a 40-foot craft accompanying the swimmer.

GETTING TO KNOW THE COURSE

There are numerous questions you need to have answered about a course before any open water swim. Some information you will need to know includes

☑ how many buoys or markers are on the course, and what color they are;

☑ how many yards are between each buoy;

☑ whether there is a turnaround buoy and, if so, the color;

☑ if the course is an out and back, on what side the swimmer needs to stay;

☑ if the turnaround marker is a boat, that the boat is marked and it is secure;

☑ information about the start and finish, such as if there is a run into and out of the water;

☑ what the exact finish point is;

☑ if the swim is parallel to shore, what type of land and water markers are there;

☑ how many heats there will be;

☑ whether the race is divided by age and/or sex.

For a swim under three miles, whether it is a triathlon or an open water swim, few races allow a swimmer to use a support craft. In this situation it is the swimmer's responsibility to guide himself or herself. Normally, the race committee has outlined a rough course on the entry form (figure 4.1, *a* and *b*).

While much of this information may be on the entry form or there may be a number to call for more information, this information may not be readily available until race day. To answer these questions prior to race day, initially contact the race committee, who should have a person you can question. If not, ask the committee to recommend a swimmer you can talk to who has raced the event in the past. Have your questions prepared ahead of time to save time and to make sure each of your questions gets answered.

If the course is over three miles, hire a boat to drive the course and study the start and finish points before the race. You and your coach should study the course, go over major markers, and check for currents or potentially challenging sections. In most

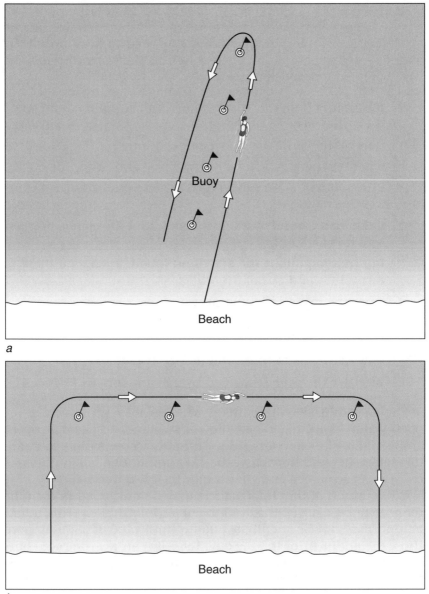

a

b

Figure 4.1 (*a*) An out-and-back course and (*b*) a parallel-to-shore course.

international races, the race committee provides a boat to survey the course.

The briefing before the swim answers many questions, but, ideally, a few days before the race, try to swim on the racecourse or a similar course to help you and your coach acclimatize to the course. If possible, have a kayaker or paddler accompany you on a short swim to help you locate major markers on the beach—distinctive houses, telephone poles, radio wires, piers, lifeguard towers, fast-food restaurant signs, etc.—to assist your navigation. The location of the swim will dictate whether this is possible. In some races, the course is not set up until race day, and in other areas there is too much boat traffic to allow for practices. In these instances, it is imperative to arrive at check-in at least an hour and a half before the swim begins. This time allows you to study the course, check for markers, and complete a warm-up swim.

VISUAL TECHNIQUES

If the swim is to a fixed point in the middle of a lake or the ocean, you might not have any markers other than those the race committee provides. Know how many buoys there are, so you limit how many times you need to lift your head to search for the turnaround or the finish. There may be a turnaround boat with a tall mast that you can see in the distance; however, if there is fog, you may not be able to see the boat.

Relying on the Lead Boat or Swimmers

Some races may have a lead boat. If you are in the lead and fast enough, you can follow it, but try not to lift your head very often; limit lifting your head to once every 300 to 400 yards. If you are not fast enough to see the lead boat clearly, then you are probably in the middle of the pack. To stay on the right course, follow the bubbles from the swimmer in front of you, and try to keep at least a foot between you and the bubbles. If you don't, you may accidentally hit the foot of the swimmer in front of you. Some swimmers can't stand having their feet touched or dragging another swimmer.

If you are close enough to see bubbles, then the first swimmer is dragging you or you are drafting off of him. Beware, this swimmer might retaliate; watch for him to pull his legs up to kick you in the face. This could knock off your goggles or do other damage. Also watch out for a swimmer who drops his legs to let you ride up over them; then as soon as you are near his hips he kicks up as hard as he can. This is extremely painful and can knock the wind out of you. This type of incident usually happens

at the beginning of mass races. Remember, not all hits or kicks are on purpose. If you are careful and accidentally hit someone, lift your head up and swim a few strokes in place for a second to prevent being kicked intentionally by the person you just hit.

To help stay on course, you can also watch the swimmers on both sides of you. If one lifts her head quite often, use this information. If the swimmer is on course, she probably won't make any corrections. If she makes corrections constantly, don't follow her. Let the other swimmers lift their heads; conserve your energy. If you are nervous swimming in crowded conditions, practice swimming with a group. This can be done in the ocean or in a lane in the pool. With practice, you can feel more comfortable in a group and ultimately relax during a race.

Relying on Predetermined Markers

If you have chosen major markers, you should be able to see them when you turn your head to breathe to save you from lifting your head. If you are swimming in the ocean, time your breathing to roll with the crest or peak of the wave. This action puts you higher than the still-water line and makes it easier to see the shore and your markers, which will help you stay on course.

CRAFT-ASSISTED NAVIGATION

For a race where a small craft such as a paddleboard, kayak, canoe, or rowboat is used, you need to follow a few guidelines. (For a discussion of each type of craft, refer to chapter 3.) First, if this is a USS or FINA race, you must stay three meters away from the side or back of the craft. There are no similar rules for triathlons (although there are rules against drafting in the bike portion of a triathlon). A second rule followed by all organizations is that the swimmer may not touch the support craft or the crew. (In chapter 9 the feeding for a swim from a support craft will be explained in detail.)

The craft may be used to hide you from your competition, if it stays a bit behind you or is on the opposite side of most of the other swimmers. This can assist you in making a move on the field or changing course.

The paddler or steerer who is in charge of the support craft must steer the straightest course, so you can simply follow the direction of the craft. Normally, as a swimmer, you will want to be between the bow and middle of the craft to ensure that you can maintain eye contact with your coach or support person on board. The paddler or steerer will situate the craft next to you. You should not have to find the craft; rather, the craft should find you. Prior to the swim, the paddler or steerer should tell you where he or she will pick you up and on what side the boat will be. A few extra feet of swimming could cost you the race, so you should not have to swim to the craft.

In most instances, you will want to be on the shore side of the craft (figure 4.2a). This positioning not only gives you the shore and the craft to watch, but also protects you from rough seas. If the wind is blowing off the shore or if waves are hitting from the other side, then the craft can take the inside or upwind course (figure 4.2b).

Powerboats

If your support vehicle is a powerboat, the driver has a few more problems to deal with on a swim. Besides keeping the boat next to you and steering a straight course, the driver needs to be aware of the fumes emitted from the craft. To ensure that you

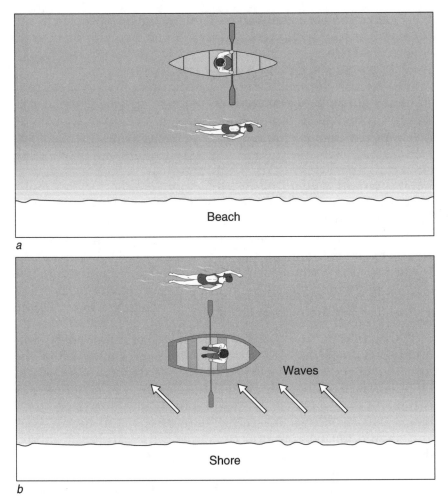

a

b

Figure 4.2 (a) Swimmer between a beach and support craft, and (b) a support craft between waves and the swimmer.

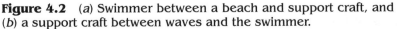

aren't smelling the fumes, the driver *must* keep the craft downwind of you. In fog, the fumes sit on the water, and the driver will have to keep the boat further from you. You must be protected from the fumes, so that you do not get sick due to even short exposure to diesel fumes. Once you throw up, dehydration and hypothermia are a danger.

In the third hour of my Channel crossing, the wind had picked up significantly, and the navigator decided to move me to the other side of the boat so the boat would break the waves. Within five minutes of swimming on this side, I began to smell the fumes of the boat. It was easier to swim on this side, but I had to move back to the other side because the fumes were making me sick. This choice added time to the crossing, but if I had become sick, I may not have been able to complete the swim.

The engine blades of a powerboat can also pose a danger to a swimmer. Both the driver and the coach must watch that the swimmer does not drop behind the boat or veer into the boat. If this happens, the driver must put the engine into neutral until the swimmer's course is corrected. At a feeding, if the swimmer moves next to the craft, again the engine must be put into neutral. Once the swimmer moves away, then and only then should the driver put the boat in gear. If the driver tries to steer away from the swimmer, the stern of the boat will swing into the swimmer's path. If the driver heads into the swimmer, the bow might hit the swimmer. These are examples of why the swimmer needs to leave first and the boat follow. For extra safety, the engine should have a propeller guard.

As with the three-meter rule with a boat, swimmers must stay at least three meters away from other swimmers. This rule prevents one swimmer from drafting off another in a race. This rule is only enforced in national or international races when the distance is 10 miles or longer. In the shorter open water races and in triathlons, one swimmer will draft off of another swimmer. Each boat must also stay out of the way of other boats' swimmers, which can be challenging at the beginning of a long race. Some longer race events help alleviate this situation by not allowing the craft to pick up the swimmer until after the one-mile mark. In addition to both of these rules, for the first two kilometers from the start, at any turn, and at the finish, the three-meter rule is disregarded. If a boat deliberately cuts off another swimmer, the race committee can disqualify that boat's swimmer.

CIRCUIT COURSES

In a circuit course, there tends to be more drafting. Since the course is constricted, it is easier to draft off another swimmer. Since there are two to four turns in a circuit course, the three-meter rule is not followed for a significant part of the swim. This is the typical course for lakes and shorter triathlons (figure 4.3).

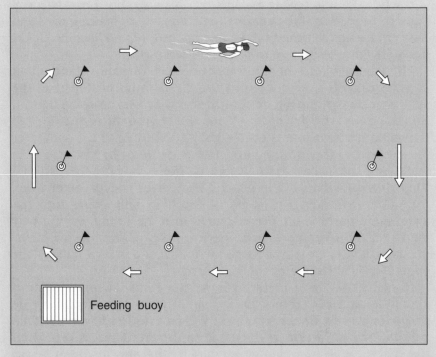

Figure 4.3 A circuit course.

When the three-meter rule does not apply, follow the stern of the craft by a few feet, which offers you a significant draft (though there is added danger from blades and fumes if the craft is engine-powered). If this is not possible, you may follow a flag hung off the back of the boat.

Large Craft

For a larger craft, 20- to 70-foot or longer, swim between the middle of the boat and the stern, since it is too difficult for the navigator on a larger vessel to have the swimmer in the front half of the boat. If you veer into the boat's course, the boat could easily run over you.

For a daylight swim, you can rely on the boat to navigate for you. If there are fumes—which are much more significant from a larger craft—the vessel can switch sides with you. Most larger vessels have a light system rigged for the middle of the boat for the swimmer to use as a guide during a night swim. If you are afraid of the dark, such a system will light the water sufficiently. The negative part of this light is that it attracts fish. Therefore, this light should not be too bright, or you might stay farther away from the boat and therefore further away from the interested fish. The best type of light is a 500- to 1,000-watt floodlight, which allows you to see the light (though you only see shadows on the boat).

Kayak or Paddleboard Assistance

On certain swims when a large boat is used, a kayak or a paddleboard is also used for support by staying next to the swimmer and setting a course off of the main boat. This option is beneficial for monitoring the swimmer's face and stroke. If there is a problem with illness or hypothermia, it is easier to pick up the swimmer. If there is a problem with marine life or another boat, the large boat can maneuver to deal with the problem and leave the swimmer with enough support. When the swimmer is fed, these smaller crafts can guide the swimmer while the bigger boat is shifting out of neutral. A fast swimmer can take off very

quickly after eating and leave the boat behind quickly. If the swimmer is off course, it could cost the swimmer time and distance to correct for this. Many times, after eating is when the swimmer will veer in front of the boat, forcing the navigator to delay the boat's start. Again, this can mean a large course correction, but with the small craft support, the paddler can use a compass to keep the swimmer on course.

BEING PREPARED

There is always a chance a craft will sink or an engine will break down during a race or swim. Prepare for this and remember to head in the proper direction, and keep swimming while the paddler, navigator, or the race committee remedy the situation. In some races, you would be given a new boat or paddler. If a coach is with you, the coach should keep an eye on you and keep pointing in your direction. If a major problem arises, the coach should immediately call for help by radio, waving an extended hand overhead, or blowing a whistle or horn. Some races provide flags; some ask the person to stand up and wave with both hands—the international signal for help. Your support crew should know which system you are using and should be able to tell the rescue people the direction and time of last sighting you to help the rescuers calculate the distance you may have covered in that time.

If you are swimming an individual crossing, do not swim away from a disabled boat if there is no smaller craft support. This is not only dangerous but also foolish. If there is fog, you could be lost and never found. If you have problems, there would be no way to help. If a swim has to be terminated because there is no other way to support you, terminate the swim. Your life and safety are more important than any swim.

NAVIGATIONAL SYSTEMS

There are five types of navigational systems: the line-of-sight, the marine compass, the Loran, the hand-held GPS, and the GPS with the Huisveld marking system. This last system is the GPS system that Pete Huisveld adapted into a better system. One of the best books on navigation is David Burch's *Funda-*

mentals of Kayak Navigation, which explains four of the five navigational systems in more detail than here. This information may be helpful for craft-assisted swims. The line-of-sight navigational system is used in a noncraft-assisted swim or leg of a triathlon.

Line-of-Sight Navigation

The simplest and most frequently used form of navigation in open water is line-of-sight navigation. This method is simply aiming at the destination without any concern for your location. If you just keep pointed at the destination, you will eventually get there. However, this method of navigation can be rather inefficient. In a short swim or a leg of a triathlon, a swimmer should follow the markers or guide off of other swimmers to stay on course unless there is an easy line-of-sight finish.

Knowledge of location is a problem that mariners have faced for thousands of years. The traditional method requires accurate knowledge of time and skill in the use of a sextant to take star sightings. Today's technology has provided an easier solution: the Global Positioning System (GPS), discussed in detail below.

Traditional open water navigation is line-of-sight navigation and is easy assuming the destination is visible. Unfortunately, it can also be very inefficient. Figure 4.4 represents a swim across the San Pedro Channel to Catalina Island. The best swim would be the straight line, which covers about 21 statute miles. Assuming no outside factors affect the swim, line-of-sight navigation will follow that line. The San Pedro Channel is one of the better swims for making the "no outside factors" assumption since there are no significant currents like there are in the English Channel. Waves are possible though unlikely (similar to a lake swim). There will likely be a 10 mile per hour wind out of the west (very likely a gentle breeze). The average swim speed is two to two and a half miles per hour (very fast; to date only five swimmers have been able to cross the San Pedro Channel at over two and a half miles per hour and no one has made it as fast as three miles per hour). Finally, line-of-sight navigation is used. If these assumptions are followed the swim will follow the curved course in figure 4.4 instead of the straight course.

The reason the swim will not follow the straight-line course is fairly simple. The boat will continue to drift east of the desired course until the force of the wind pushing east equals the force

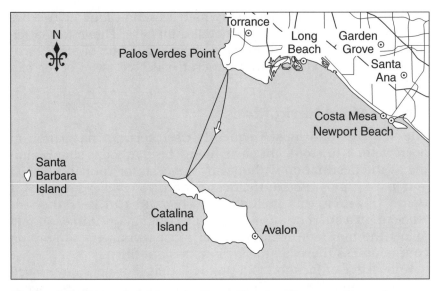

Figure 4.4 Line-of-sight navigation will naturally cause the swimmer to take a curved route across the San Pedro Channel.

of the boat's engine pushing west. Without going into the trigonometry of this situation, suffice it to say that the boat must actually aim west of the intended destination in order to track a straight course. The boat must fight the force of the wind, and the only way it can do that is by pointing into the wind at some unknown angle.

During this hypothetical swim, the breeze out of the west steadily pushes on the slow-moving boat escorting the swimmer. This slow but steady push to the east is what will cause the swim to follow the curved line. Carefully plotting this out on a map reveals that the swim went approximately two miles further than it should have. A simple calculation shows that the swimmer will swim 42 to 50 minutes longer than if he had swum a straight course. If the swimmer is slower than assumed, the effect of the wind will cause the swim to cover an even longer distance.

It would be a shame if a swim across the San Pedro Channel missed breaking a record by over half an hour because line-of-sight navigation forced the swim to be two miles longer than necessary. It would be an even greater shame if a swimmer did not complete a swim because he became exhausted, having to swim several miles farther than he had planned. We'll return to this example again below.

Marine Compass

For smaller craft such as a paddleboard or a kayak, a marine compass may be helpful. In many cases, the craft is low in the water, making line-of-sight navigation difficult. As long as the navigator knows the direction you need to head, he or she can use the compass if the navigator knows the direction *before* the swim begins and can point the bow of the craft to that reading and continue paddling. However, the navigator may need to check the compass every once in a while to make sure you are still on course. Remember, the waves, tides, or currents could push you off of the proper course. Also, a compass is especially useful in fog.

A marine compass has 360 degrees. Unlike the compass you may have used when hiking, you can read a marine compass by pointing it toward the sight you are aiming for or toward the bow, if you can't see the land. On a marine compass, the numbers don't move, so when the needle moves, the numbers remain stationary and the needle points to the direction you are heading. Since charts only use the magnetic north, you don't have to worry about the true north and the compass corrections, since this is different for a land compass. When using a marine compass for navigation, turn the bow in line with the compass heading, find a reference point, and keep it on the same side of the bow. If you don't have a reference mark or if it is covered with fog, you will have to rely on the compass for direction.

Loran System

The Loran system is a land-based navigation system operated by the Coast Guard and isn't as accurate as the GPS system detailed below. Most older boats have this system, and the navigator knows how to use it. Since few coaches or swimmers need to know this system, I will not describe it further.

Global Positioning System

GPS is a highly accurate method of determining your position anywhere on the planet. The system consists of a receiver and a couple of dozen satellites placed in orbit around the earth by the United States government. The sole purpose of the satellite is to transmit navigational information. The part of the system discussed here is the hand-held receiver, which is generally the size of a small transistor radio. In 1988, you couldn't obtain one. By 1992, you could find one for about $1,000 (US) if you really worked at it, and by 1996, they were quite easy to find for as little as $200 (US).

A hand-held GPS receiver allows accurate knowledge of your position anywhere on earth at any time. Depending on the individual unit, the system has many other features that can assist with open water navigation. Since those options depend on the individual unit, they are addressed here only briefly.

Hand-held GPS receivers are extremely user-friendly. A new receiver needs to be turned on for 15 to 20 minutes to let it search for satellites and determine its location. If the location of the receiver is changed by more than 3,000 miles since the last time it was operated, it will be a little confused. For example, if the receiver was in Los Angeles, California, the last time it was used and then moved to Rome, Italy, when the receiver is turned on, it will look for satellites above the horizon in Los Angeles. It will not be able to receive any radio transmissions from Rome. After a few minutes of trying to communicate with satellites on the opposite side of the world, it will give up and start the same kind of satellite search that it did when it was first turned on. After these two conditions (giving 20 minutes and reorienting if the location has changed) are taken into account, all you honestly have to know about GPS technology is how to change your receiver's batteries and how to turn it on!

A GPS receiver has a small display screen (figure 4.5). It will probably display information about ground track, ground speed, and altitude. Don't worry about these readings, since they aren't important for navigating in an open water swim. What is important to know is where you are on the surface of the planet. This reading will look something like

N33° 44.213'

W118° 24.350'

While GPS information has made knowledge of current position easy, you do need to know what to do with this information. The letters and numbers are the latitude and longitude of a position. In the example above, that position is 33 degrees, 44.213 minutes north of the equator and 118 degrees, 24.350 minutes west of Greenwich, England. By itself, this fact may not be very useful. However, when combined with a good nautical navigation chart, you have a very powerful piece of navigational information.

Figure 4.5 A hand-held Global Positioning System (GPS) receiver.

If you are not used to using circular or spherical coordinates, units of degrees and minutes may seem strange. However, these measures are the international standard. Basically, a circle is divided into 360 degrees, and each degree is divided into 60 minutes. Using these units, one circle around the earth to the north and south and one to the east and west allows accurate determination on the surface of the sphere known as earth. With just a little practice, it becomes easy to use.

Nautical charts are available for nearly all navigable waters throughout the world. The U.S. Department of Commerce and the National Oceanic and Atmospheric Administration (NOAA) distribute charts for U.S. waters. American charts for foreign waters are published by the Defense Mapping Agency and are generally available from NOAA chart distributors. Along the top, bottom, and sides of these maps are latitude and longitude markings. Use these markings to plot your position, based on the readings from the GPS receiver.

Now let's return to our example of navigating a swim across the San Pedro Channel. If you use GPS to navigate, you can maintain the straight-line course. The GPS position information allows course corrections early in a swim to keep on a straight course. The secret to doing this lies in knowledge of current position versus desired position. Using the NOAA chart for the San Pedro Channel and N33° 44.213', W118° 24.350', plot the position (see figure 4.6). This, with just a little practice, is fairly easy.

Across the top and bottom of the chart are markings for 117° 30', 118°, and 118° 30'. (Figure 4.6 is only part of the total chart, so it shows only 118° 30', 118° 25', and 118° 20'.) Between these markings, there are markings every five minutes: 05', 10', 15', etc. Between each of these, there are bars representing each individual minute and then markings for each tenth of a minute (see figure 4.7).

Across the sides of the chart are markings for 33° 20' and 33° 40'. (Figure 4.6 only shows 33° 40' and 33° 45'.) Each individual minute and tenth of a minute is marked the same way, as shown in figure 4.7.

Draw a straight line down from 118° 24.350' and another straight line across from 33° 44.213' (see figure 4.8). Where the two lines meet is your position. In this example the position is

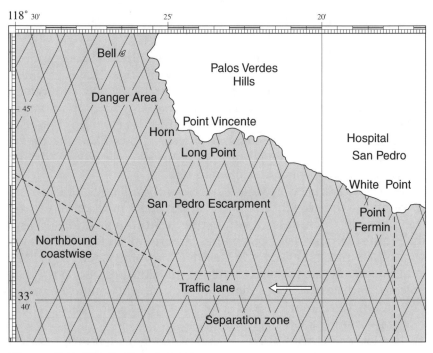

Figure 4.6 Navigational charts.

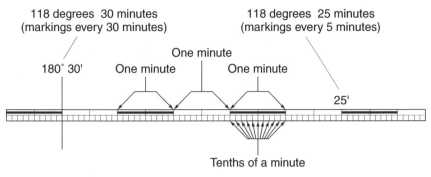

Figure 4.7 GPS markings.

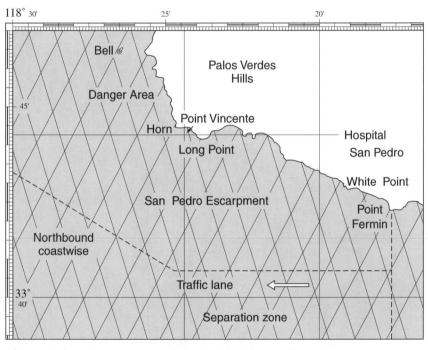

Figure 4.8 Starting point at Point Vicente, California.

just off of the beach south of Point Vicente, California, a good place to start a swim to Catalina Island.

The GPS system can be used anywhere in the world without a permit or license, which makes the system ideal. If you hire a navigator who does not have a GPS, borrow or find a GPS for your navigator. Before the swim, instruct the navigator to take a reading every 30 minutes to prevent you from swimming extra miles.

Huisveld's Improvement of GPS

Using this NOAA chart of the San Pedro Channel, simply draw a straight line from the starting point to the intended finishing point (figure 4.9, the straight line). If the navigator considers

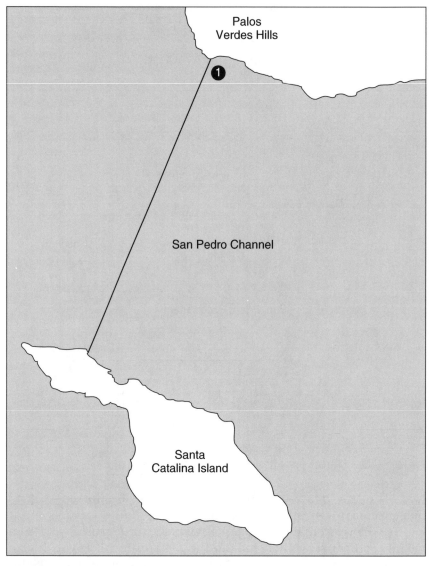

Figure 4.9 Route for crossing the San Pedro Channel.

point one of figure 4.9 (30 minutes into a swim, assuming three miles per hour) he or she knows very early into the swim that you are off course. At this point he or she can make a correction of the boat's course to the west and you only swim a few extra yards instead of extra miles.

By plotting the position on the chart every half hour, the navigator can continue to make course corrections to keep you close to the desired straight-line course. One potential problem is that when you tell the boat captain, who is usually quite experienced, to make a course correction, he or she might simply say the boat is right on course. However, showing the captain a GPS receiver and position plot indicating that the boat is, in fact, off of the desired course will make your point.

The above plotting is the Huisveld improvement. Taking a reading every 30 minutes accounts for water conditions and the swimmer's speed. The GPS has its own navigational programming, and the user must read the receiver's owner's manual to determine how to program it. The following is a simple summary of what the navigator should be able to perform.

In the navigation mode, the navigator needs to enter into the receiver's memory the intended destination. For the hypothetical swim to Catalina Island, the coordinates to enter are N33° 28.3', W118° 31.8'. This is the closest point from Point Vicente, on Catalina Island, where you can safely go ashore. In the navigation mode, a GPS receiver will now tell the navigator the direction you need to go and the direction you are actually going. With this information, course corrections can be made quickly and easily. The navigator doesn't need a chart but still needs to check the GPS every 30 minutes and have the captain make corrections, if necessary.

In 1995, Pete Huisveld's father had a hand-held GPS system on Pete's Catalina crossing. Thirty minutes into the swim, his father knew Pete was slightly off course. He told the navigator and showed him the reading. The navigator was using the Loran system but was not making corrections. He was basically using line-of-sight navigation. However, he made the correction and checked with Pete's father every half hour for the rest of the swim.

ACCOUNTING FOR WEATHER, TIDES, AND CURRENTS

When navigating a swim, take the weather into consideration. If there is a cross wind, you should swim diagonally into the wind. If there is a head wind, you should head into it. If there is an off-shore wind, swimming closer to the shore may be easier. In a following wind, you will be pushed forward; take advantage of the wave and ride it forward. In windy weather, an anchored boat should face into the wind telling you the direction the wind is blowing. Whenever possible, the support boat should be between the swimmer and the poor weather.

If the swim may be affected by the tides, know when high and low tides will occur. There are two high and low tides a day. In a tide, the water rushes in (high tide), calms down (slack water), then moves out (low tide). If the water is building up, it is the flood part of the tide; if it is slowing down, it is the ebb part of the tide. The navigator should be able to see a tide change if you are close to the shore. If there is a current in the river, lake, or ocean, the navigator should check for an anchored boat which will always point into the water flow. If you are swimming against the current or in a river affected by tides, swimming as close to shore as possible is best, since the currents are not as strong there.

Depending on the size of the support craft, use a compass or a GPS hand-held system to assist in navigation. Let the navigator be in charge of this, so you can focus on your swim. Just as it is important to navigate efficiently, it is equally important to use proper stroke techniques to swim as efficiently as possible. You will learn about proper stroke technique in chapter 5.

5

Technique Tips for the Open Water

Prior to the 1950s, two strokes were used in open water swimming: breaststroke and freestyle. Breast-stroke is a slow but enduring stroke and is rarely used anymore. Freestyle is the most popular style for open water swimming, because it is faster and more efficient. However, the stroke used for sprinting and distance freestyle in a pool is different than open water freestyle.

OPEN WATER FREESTYLE

Open water freestyle has three objectives: speed, efficiency, and endurance. Depending on the length of the swim, one objective may be emphasized more than the other two. For example, in triathlon distances up to 2.4 miles and open water swims of 3.1 miles (5 K), the most important objective is speed.

Speed

Speed is achieved with proper stroke mechanics and a fast turnover. The stroke turnover is determined by counting the number of times the arms are pulled, or turned over, in a minute. For

© Mike Griggs

pool swimmers, the rate is calculated by counting both arm pulls as one. In open water, each single arm pull is counted as one, which means your open water stroke rate is double your pool stroke rate. A prevailing belief is that open water swimmers cannot maintain the rapid arm turnover used by pool swimmers, due to the longer distances swum in open water. For example, the longest pool event world record is under 15 minutes, while the 16-mile world championship record is around 5 hours and the English Channel record is over 7 hours. With proper training, however, the difference in stroke rate over these distances should be negligible. As U.S. national coach, my goal for the swimmers was to achieve a consistent stroke rate over all distances. The swimmers were able to achieve this goal through hard work over a few years. The ideal turnover rate for a swimmer in open water of a distance of a mile or more should be the same stroke rate that the swimmer uses during a 1500-meter pool swim. This is the goal, and periodically the swimmer can swim a 1500-meter race in the pool and try to maintain the same stroke rate throughout. This stroke rate is different for each swimmer. In time, swimmers should be able to maintain their own stroke rate for any distance.

The turnover for a sprint event, such as the 50 meters, is a few strokes per minute faster than the 1500-meter turnover. In open water swimming, the average male's turnover used to be 40 to 70 strokes per minute, and the female's was a little higher. In recent years, however, with the influx of pool swimmers into open water swimming, the male's average is now in the high 70s and low 80s, while the female's is in the high 80s and even the low 90s, as measured in open water terms.

While training six to eight hours a day for the English Channel swim, my goal was to maintain 88 strokes per minute for the whole swim. I tried to think of the English Channel swim as a 200-meter swim in the Olympics. It was a sprint. As the swim began, my stroke count was 92 strokes per minute. One of the sanctioning officials on the boat went over to my mother and told her I would not be able to maintain this high stroke count for the whole swim. He said he had been on quite a few record swims and knew what he was talking about. My mother very nicely stated, "I'm sorry, but you don't know my daughter." For the next seven and a half hours, I maintained 89 to 92 strokes per minute. The excitement of the swim helped me maintain this high stroke rate. After I completed the swim, the official came over to my mother and said, "Mrs. Dean, you were right. I didn't know your daughter." Maintaining a consistent stroke count is imperative for a successful swim.

Efficiency

For races of 4 to 10 miles, speed and efficiency are of primary importance, and endurance plays a tertiary role. Efficiency of stroke ensures that the least amount of energy is expended in each sequence of the stroke. To have efficiency in the stroke there are five components which need to be perfected. This is the same whether you are in the pool or open water. These components will be discussed later in this chapter.

Endurance

Endurance is the ability to swim continuously in an economical and effective manner for a number of miles or hours. For swims between 10 and 20 miles, endurance plays a greater role, though speed and efficiency are still vital objectives. This is especially true in the open water world championship distance of 16 miles (25 K). For swims over 20 miles, the primary objective is endurance.

FIVE COMPONENTS OF FREESTYLE

Freestyle can be divided into five components: body position, rolling, arm movement, leg movement, and breathing. These stroke components are the same for pool or open water freestyle.

Body Position

The most beneficial body position for freestyle is streamlined. This means the head, shoulders, and hips are in a straight line, producing less drag (figure 5.1). If one body part is out of alignment, the resulting drag will slow you down.

A few drills can improve your swimming body position. The first streamlining drill starts by standing on the deck, extending your arms over your head, placing your left hand on top of your right hand, squeezing your upper arms into your head and ears, and tightening your thighs together. Next, perform this drill while lying on the surface of the water. Once you have achieved proper alignment, start kicking. Gradually add your arm stroke.

If you try dropping your legs from the surface while stroking, you should be able to feel how much tougher it is to swim. Likewise, if you drop your head toward your chest, you should feel how much more difficult swimming becomes. After a length, re-elevate your head position to find the most comfortable and efficient body position.

Another drill to perform in a pool is to push off of the wall in a streamlined position. Stay in this position until you stop moving

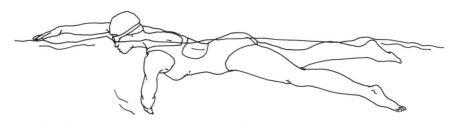

Figure 5.1 Maintaining a streamlined alignment of head, shoulders, and hips reduces drag.

forward. Next, push off of the wall again, but this time drop your legs as in the above drill. Then push off and drop your head. Next push off and lift your head. Lifting and dropping your head should produce drag. In each drill, you should sense which position feels the most comfortable and efficient.

In most cases, the head will be tilted slightly upward, approximately 1 to 10 degrees. This upward tilt allows you to look ahead with your eyes. In a pool with lines running perpendicular to your direction, you should be able to see at least one line in front of you. In the open water, you should be able to see a few feet in front of you. The water level, whether in the pool or in open water, should be an inch or so above your forehead. In salt water, the head may be a bit higher, perhaps a half inch.

Body Roll

The second component of efficient freestyle is the body roll, which can help you get the most out of your stroke. The most efficient rolling action consists of moving your body along the long axis (figure 5.2). Imagine your long axis as a pole running through your head from the top, down your spine, and exiting the groin; since you cannot bend in the middle, your body needs to rotate around this pole. As you roll your body into the swimming stroke, you will use more of your body's large muscles—including your powerful back muscles—in the pull. Also, rolling aids in the arm recovery above the surface of the water and facilitates breathing. In choppy conditions in open water, an exaggerated roll can mean the difference between getting a breath of air or not. Finally, the roll helps the hips rotate, and this rotation assists the legs in kicking.

Aim for a roll of 30 to 70 degrees along the axis. This allows the entering arm to extend in front of the head and deeper in the

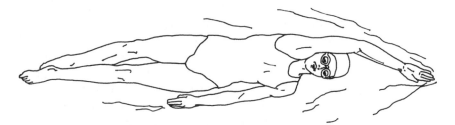

Figure 5.2 To roll efficiently, rotate on an imaginary pole running the length of your torso. A roll of 30 to 70 degrees allows full arm extension and a strong pull.

water, resulting in a stronger pull.

There are numerous drills to help rolling. The best is to combine kicking, streamlining, and rolling. The first stage is to kick on one side, with your head in streamlined position, your left hand over your head, and your right arm at your side (figure 5.3). Kick 20 times with both legs, take a pull with your left arm while you breathe to the right, recover with your right arm, and roll to your other side. At this point, kick 20 more times while taking a pull with your right arm and recovering with your left arm. Continue alternating sides in this manner for 200 meters. Then repeat the drill and reduce the number of kicks by four with each 200-meter repeat. Once you are down to three kicks with each side, stop the drill, since this is the regular stroke. Another variation is to start this drill with six kicks and drop to three on each side.

Figure 5.3 The sidekicking drill can help you perfect your roll.

Arm Pull

In distance freestyle, the arms are the primary means of propulsion. The arms use a slanted *Z* or an *S* pattern pull underwater, followed by an above-water recovery. The stroke can be divided into five phases: the entry; the downsweep (down and out); the insweep (in, back, and up); the outsweep (down, out, and through); and the recovery.

One of the most important points about the arm pull is to keep your fingers to the elbow in a straight line. This portion of your arm should not bend or bend only slightly at the wrist. A large bend at your wrist means that the only muscles you can use are your forearms. However, if your wrist is only slightly bent, then you can use not only your forearm muscles but also your arm and shoulder muscles. If you use a proper roll, your back muscles also contribute. A slight bend of the wrist allows for a scull, diagonal pull, in the stroke.

A second important rule concerning the arm pull is to make sure your elbow is always higher than your fingertips. It is important that each phase of the stroke should gradually flow from one to the other, and that the arm speed increases throughout the stroke. During the entry phase, your arm moves forward; during the downsweep your hand speed increases and continues to increase through the insweep, reaching its fastest speed during the powerful outsweep.

Entry. The first phase of the arm stroke is the entry (figure 5.4, *a* and *b*). Your hand should enter the water before your elbow (elbow is higher) and should be extended in front of your head while being angled forward and slightly downward (see figure 5.4*a*). As stated earlier, the roll helps your arm extend in front of your head. Your extended hand should be 6 to 10 inches under the surface of the water, with your fingers comfortably together (though some separation is natural and the amount of separation will vary from swimmer to swimmer) (figure 5.4*b*). Keep your fingers parallel to the surface or angled slightly, with your thumb a little downward, and keep your elbow slightly higher than your hand. If your hand is higher than your elbow, your elbow must have dropped. If this occurs, you will have less power in the

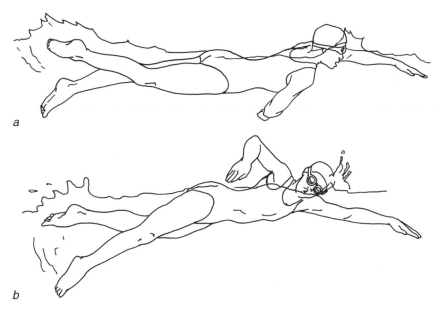

a

b

Figure 5.4 Arm stroke phase—arm entry; (*a*) entry showing the hand-to-elbow position (with the elbow above the hand) and (*b*) entry with extended hand and arm in front of the face; the hand is six inches below water surface.

downsweep and the insweep.

To drill hand entry, repeat the drill for rolling described earlier in this chapter, and pay attention to your hand entry. This drill gives you time to feel your hand extension and pay attention to the depth of your hand entry. As you reduce the number of kicks, continue to pay attention to your entry extension and depth.

Downsweep. The second phase of the arm pull is the downsweep (see figure 5.5, *a-c*). In this phase, press your hand downward and outward in one motion, a diagonal scull. The downward distance is about a foot, while the outward is four to six inches

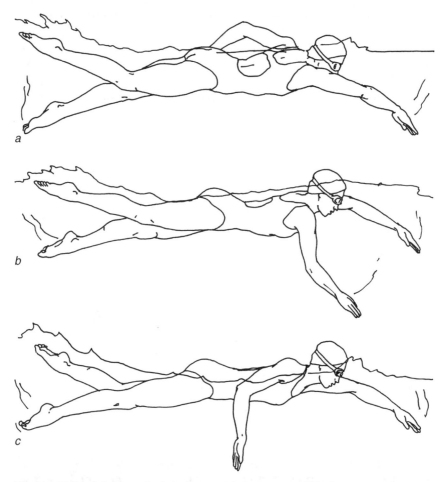

Figure 5.5 (*a*) Arm stroke phase—downsweep; (*b*) downsweep showing the right hand down and out, the body flat, and the left hand up; and (*c*) downsweep with hand switching and recovery under water.

from the center of your body to just inside your shoulder. Your elbow only moves slightly backward as the down and out hand pull occurs.

A drill to practice your downsweep uses the Red Cross beginning swim stroke, a half freestyle stroke with an underwater recovery. In this stroke, you extend your hand forward and under the water. Follow this movement with the downsweep (figure 5.5, *b* and *c*). Your hand is then recovered forward and underwater. With this drill, the beginning swim stroke, make sure to roll your body. Work your arms alternately and use a kick to maintain proper body position.

Insweep. During the insweep (figure 5.6, *a* and *b*), turn your hand inward and sweep upward to or past the center of your body, with your hand leading your elbow. Your elbow bend should range from 130 to 100 degrees during this phase. Your hand ends up under your chest but about eight inches below your body. For women, the hand passes through the center of the body. For men, the hand rarely pulls past the center.

To drill the insweep, start with your hands in downsweep phase and rotate your hand into the insweep. After this pull, extend your hands forward and outward and repeat. It is best if you can do this drill while swimming above a black line in a pool, so that you can center your head on the black line. Start your pull outside

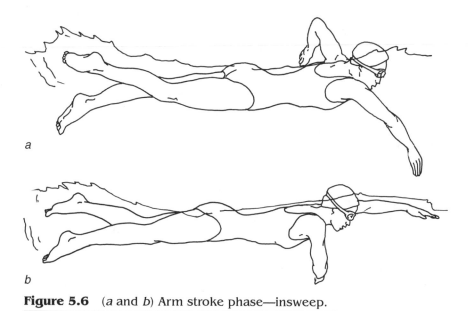

a

b

Figure 5.6 (*a* and *b*) Arm stroke phase—insweep.

the black line and finish in the center or just past the center of the black line.

Outsweep. The fourth phase of the freestyle arm stroke is the outsweep, also known as the upsweep in Ernie Maglisco's *Swimming Even Faster*. This phase, the most powerful phase of the stroke, involves pressing your hand downward, outward, and backward toward your hip and letting your hand lead your elbow (figure 5.7, *a-c*). During this part of the stroke, your wrist bends to allow your hand a little snap at the end of your stroke. In rough water or as you become fatigued, you may not press as far as in flat conditions or when you are not fatigued. You should touch the side of your leg, mid thigh, every once in a while to ensure the outsweep is completed properly.

To drill the outsweep, start with your hand in the center of your body under your chest, the position at the end of the in-sweep. Press your hand backward toward your hip with your right arm and then left arm. Recover each arm under the water, and roll your hip out of the way of your hand as your hand reaches your hip; snap your wrist past your hip (figures 5.7, *d* and *e*).

Recovery. The final phase is recovery (figure 5.8). Lift your shoulder out of the water, followed by your elbow and, finally, your hand. Rotate your shoulder forward, hold your elbow high, and swing your hand easily forward. Once your hand passes your shoulder, your hand—never your thumb—leads the recovery. If your thumb leads, your shoulder and arm will be tight. The recovery phase needs to be a relaxing phase. In rough or wavy open water, you may have to lift your hand higher so it doesn't hit the higher water.

There is a good recovery drill that improves hand position. This drill involves recovering with your elbow high, but dragging your fingertips in the water. This drill helps you feel the high elbow and the proper position of your hand.

Kick

During an open water or distance swim, the kick is not as strong or as high as in the freestyle used for sprinting. The primary objective of kicking in open water swimming is stabilization. Many swimmers use a two-beat kick. A two-beat kick means that one kick with each leg accompanies every arm rotation, one pull with each arm. The leg kicking is the opposite leg of the arm pulling. For example, if the right arm is pulling, the left leg kicks

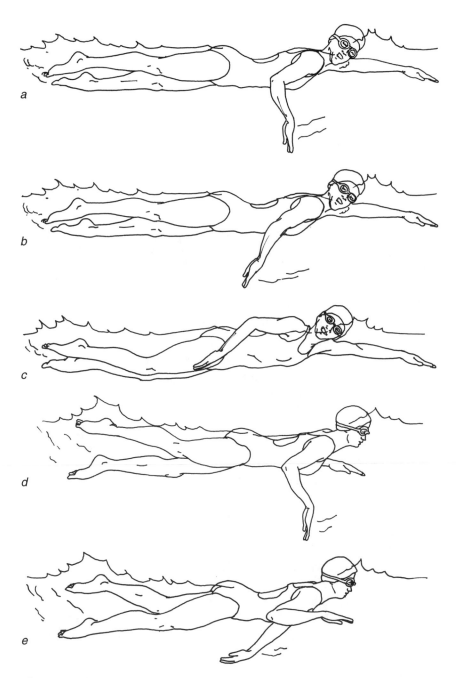

Figure 5.7 (a) Arm stroke phase—outsweep; (b) right hand under the body; the left hand at the side; (c) press the right hand out and back; recover the left arm; and (d) press the hand out and (e) back.

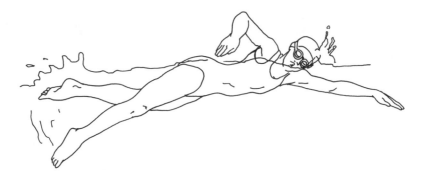

Figure 5.8 Arm stroke phase—recovery.

SHOULDER INJURIES

Shoulder injuries are common for open water swimmers. The combination of long training hours and numerous miles a week take their toll. Tendinitis of the shoulder is the most common injury. This painful injury usually occurs when the head of the humerus rubs across the biceps tendon, the supraspinatus tendon, and the coracoacromial ligament. Tendinitis causes a reduction in training time or can end a career if not properly treated. Proper stroke mechanics, ice, anti-inflammatories, rest, and deep tissue massage can help to alleviate this problem.

Pete Huisveld set a world record for men for swimming from the mainland to Catalina in 7 hours, 37 minutes, 31 seconds in 1992. In 1994 and 1995, he trained extensively to swim the channel in the opposite direction and then continue on for a double crossing. He had severe shoulder problems. He found a chiropractor, Dr. Ferrell, in Santa Barbara, who performed deep muscle massage, which was painful but worked. Pete swam pain-free for months. On the night of his crossing, rough seas battered his body. He was way ahead of the record and his shoulder did well. Unfortunately, he pinched a nerve between C6 and C7 in his spine. He had to leave the water. He courageously and intelligently listened to his body and decided the future use of his body was more important than succeeding in a swim.

downward. When the left arm is pulling, the right leg kicks downward. Since the heart can only supply a limited amount of blood to the limbs, the legs, which have numerous muscles, are used less, thus preserving the swimmer's energy.

In the last 20 years, the two-beat kick philosophy has begun to change. More and more swimmers are using a four-beat kick. The four-beat kick means two kicks with each leg per one arm pull with each arm. The four-beat kick assists in speed, especially in cold water.

In cold water, it is especially important to kick, because if you don't, after a while your hips will drop. This change in body position will cause more drag in the water, and your arms must work harder, thus slowing you down. The third and worst effect of the hips dropping is that your lower back will become cold and begin to cramp. Once this occurs, you may have to stop more often to stretch your back or you may begin to experience the first stages of hypothermia. The kick plays a major role in preventing or limiting hypothermia; therefore, the four-beat kick has to be considered in open water swimming.

Prior to swimming the English Channel, I had used a two-beat kick. As I began swimming in the 50-degree ocean in France in May, I switched to a four-beat kick because I was getting too cold. This helped me keep warm and prevented my back from cramping. For the first time in my 22 years of swimming, I really emphasized kicking, since it was vital to keeping me warm and achieving my goal of crossing the Channel.

Breathing Patterns

In open water swimming, you must maintain a regular breathing pattern. In some sprinting races, the breathing pattern changes with each length of the race. For example, at the 1996 Olympics, Amy Van Dyken of the United States used a challenging breathing pattern for her 50-meter race; she didn't take a breath until the 35-meter mark and passed her competitor at this point to win the gold medal.

The alternate breathing pattern—taking a breath every third arm stroke—is the most common and beneficial for open water swimmers. It is, however, an individual choice as to what breathing pattern is the most natural for you. When you breathe only to one side, the pull on this side may be wider, away from your body. This can create shoulder problems for both the breathing-side shoulder and the other shoulder, which has to do more work. Doing a 1,000-yard set of two lengths or a half mile straight using an alternate breathing pattern may help you fix your stroke. However, for some swimmers this change may create more problems than it fixes, so you and your coach have to weigh the advantages and the disadvantages. Moreover, since the 1990s, many of the fastest distance swimmers in the world breathe only on one side in order to breathe every stroke. This trend will likely influence the way coaches around the world train swimmers for the next decade.

Alternate breathing is beneficial to ensure not only a symmetrical stroke but also a straighter course in open water swimming. For example, if you start your stroke with your left arm (first stroke), the third stroke will also be with your left arm. To breathe on this third stroke, as your left hand touches the water, turn your head to the right with your chin turned upward toward your right shoulder. Turn your head only far enough for your mouth to clear the water, take a quick breath, look toward your shoulder, and return your chin to the water. Do not swing your eyes and chin forward (unless you are lifting your head to see where you are). After a breath is an ideal time to take a peek, because at any other time, lifting your head will cause your hips to drop.

There are many breathing patterns possible. It is important to experiment to find the one that works best for you. If you regularly use a pattern other than alternate breathing, occasionally breathe alternately to make sure you are on course and to stretch your neck muscles.

Other important techniques for efficient breathing when swimming include keeping your head in line with your body when you are not breathing. In other words, don't swing your head with your body. Second, before turning your head to breathe, exhale. Whatever air is left in your lungs needs to be blown out to ensure that you will only inhale when you turn your head. Do not waste time exhaling above the water. When you take a breath and return your head to the water, slowly exhale underwater. Many swimmers keep their mouths open all the time underwater. Strongly exhaling before turning your head to breathe will expel any water.

If open water conditions are choppy, you may only be able to breathe on one side, but knowing how to breathe alternately will still be an advantage. If you can only breathe to one side and the waves are to that side, you may be in trouble. In rough conditions, always breathe with the wave whenever possible to make breathing easier. If the wave comes from the left as it moves under your body, roll to the right and breathe. In heavy wind-pushed waves, you may have to change your breathing pattern. Sometimes conditions are so rough that the wave hits you in the head, making it difficult to breathe at all. In this case, turn your head a little further and pull your chin into your shoulder. You should be able to sneak a short breath. You need to practice this technique in training.

Once a week in an open water practice, plan a swim from the beach toward the center of the lake or out into the ocean. Do this in the afternoon when the wind may be up and conditions are rough. On the way out, breathe into the wave and on the way back breathe away from the wave. Make sure you are still in a swimming area and the area is safe from boat traffic. You can do a second loop, breathing alternately on the way in and out. On a third loop, you can alternate from breathing every stroke for 10 arm rotations to alternating breathing for 10 strokes. Attempting different breathing patterns in rough conditions will help you learn to adapt to all conditions (figure 5.9, *a* and *b*).

CORRECTING COMMON FREESTYLE ERRORS

The most common errors in freestyle are swimming with the elbow dropped and cutting the outsweep short. You and your coach need to watch constantly for the dropped-elbow error. By putting pressure on your hand throughout the stroke, you can be aware if your hand or your elbow is leading the pull. If your elbow is leading, your arm pull is less powerful. Cutting the outsweep short can be especially devastating to the most powerful phase of the arm stroke. One way to look out for this error is to touch your thigh every once in a while at the end of your outsweep. This can serve as a reminder and a stroke check.

Stroke Drills

To work on the whole stroke at once, one of the best drills is to swim one arm at a time with a kick. Drop the opposite arm (in this example, the left) to the side. If you are rolling sufficiently as your right arm is entering the water, your left arm will pop out of the water. As your downsweep begins, your left hand drops back in the water. Let your left hand move naturally. Swim 100 yards with one arm and then 100 yards with the other arm. Then swim the whole stroke, emphasizing the roll. If your left arm doesn't pop out of the water, you need to roll your body more as your right hand enters the water.

a

b

Figure 5.9 (*a*) Pete Huisveld breathing during the Catalina Crossing, and (*b*) Pete Huisveld breathing with a swell, opposite the direction of the waves.

Stroke Efficiency

To check your stroke efficiency, count the number of strokes per length of the swimming pool or a measured distance in open water. If your stroke is too flat, you may have too many strokes per length. Attempt to decrease this number by two in the next length. To do this, you will have to roll more, ride on the roll at the entry, and/or follow through stronger at your thigh. Each should help lengthen your stroke.

If you don't know how your stroke looks, you can at least figure out if it is efficient by swimming above and along a black line. As you roll into the entry, make sure your hand is above the center of the black line. As you perform the downsweep, check to see if your hand is outside of the black line. As you do the insweep, your hand should be above the center of the black line. Finally, touch the middle of your thigh with your hand at the end of the outsweep. If you have to go out of your way during the stroke to touch your thigh, your outsweep is too short. Whenever the stroke feels incorrect, you can try each of the above drills to improve it.

Ideally, a coach should watch your stroke either through an underwater window or a coach's scope (figure 5.10, *a* and *b*). The scope is put in the water, and, through it, your coach can watch or videotape your stroke. Many USS programs and colleges have this equipment, which allows a coach to watch the complete stroke. (The machine costs only $1,000 and pays for itself in one season.) With a good VCR, your coach can run the tape frame by frame and determine any problem within your stroke. It quickly demonstrates if your elbow is leading the pull or your entry or outsweep is too short.

Stroke Analysis Using the Flume

Another option is to plan a trip to the U.S. Olympic Training Center (USOTC) in Colorado Springs and arrange with the International Center for Aquatic Research to swim in the flume (figure 5.11). A biomechanist can develop force curves for each part of your stroke. These experts can demonstrate how a small correction can fix a problem and increase the force generated. Make sure you call months in advance to arrange for this unique experience, since there are limited opportunities to use the flume. (See chapter 10 for contact information.)

Figures 5.12 and 5.13 show two sets of force curves for Pete Huisveld's right arm, one done in 1991 and the other done in

a

b

Figure 5.10 (a and b) Photos of and through coach's scope.

Figure 5.11 Swimmer being tested in the flume at the U.S. Olympic Training Center in Colorado Springs, CO.

1993 at the USOTC flume. After being tested in 1991, he worked to improve the weaknesses in his stroke. By 1993, Pete had improved his hand velocity, the resultant force, propelling efficiency, and thus his overall effective force in his stroke. So, drilling your stroke and working on improving it can pay off!

OPEN WATER FLOATING

Anyone who swims in open water should know how to do a front and back float. These are important for feeding, especially if the swim is in cold water or you get cold easily. Floating will help in most rivers, lakes, and the ocean, since once you drop below three feet, the water temperature drops quickly. If you can float, you can keep your feet near the surface and stay warmer. This can be practiced weekly in an open water or pool practice by floating between sets and drinking fluids. This will simulate drinking during a long swim.

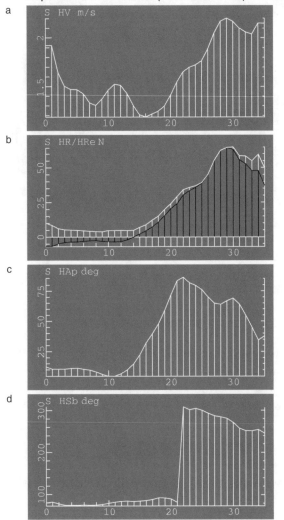

United States Swimming
International Center for Aquatic Research

AccuMotion Swimming Effectiveness Analysis
Printed August 27, 1991

Report for Pete Huisveld (file RPHUFPRE): Freestyle

Average values over the stroke:
Hand velocity: 1.651 m/s   Hand pitch angle: 38.96 deg
Resultant force: 25.54 N   Effective force: 19.33 N
Propelling efficiency: 40.08%

Figure 5.12 (*a* through *i*) Force curves for Pete Huisveld's right arm, done in 1991 at the USOTC flume.

Report for Pete Huisveld (file RPHUFPRE): Freestyle

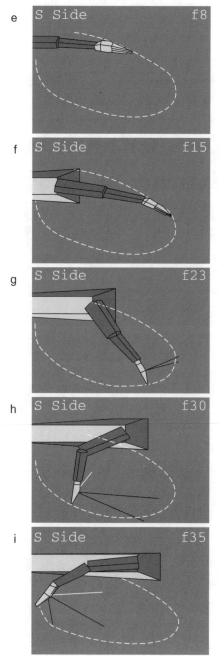

Figure 5.12 *(continued)*

United States Swimming
International Center for Aquatic Research

AccuMotion Swimming Effectiveness Analysis
Printed June 30, 1993

Report for Pete Huisveld (file RPHUF151): Freestyle

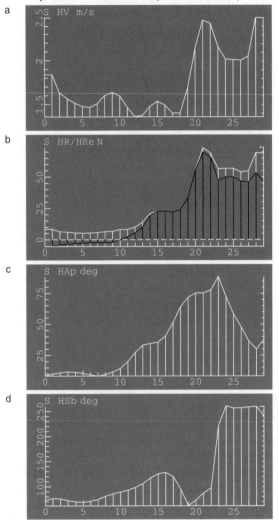

Average values over the stroke:

Hand velocity:	1.773 m/s	Hand pitch angle:	36.17 deg
Resultant force:	28.42 N	Effective force:	21.43 N
Propelling efficiency:	42.42%		

Figure 5.13 (a through i) Force curves for Pete Huisveld's right arm, done in 1993 at the USOTC flume.

Report for Pete Huisveld (file RPHUF151): Freestyle

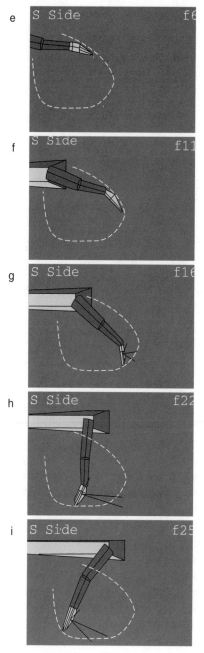

Figure 5.13 *(continued)*

HEAD-UP FREESTYLE

Another stroke you need to learn for open water swimming is the head-up freestyle. This stroke is the same as the regular freestyle, except your arm entry is shorter, your head is held up, your eyes look forward, and your mouth is kept in the water until you want to breathe. To breathe, just lift your mouth up and take a gulp of air. This stroke is beneficial when you want to see where you are or when the water is rough and is difficult to navigate. Do a few strokes of head-up freestyle and return to regular freestyle.

EGGBEATER KICK

The eggbeater kick is the final technique you need to learn as an open water swimmer. This kick allows you to be in a vertical position in the water, to keep your head above water, and to stay afloat. The eggbeater kick is similar to the breaststroke, except your legs kick alternately instead of together. Also, your chest leans forward and your knees are drawn up at a 90-degree angle to your chest.

Remember that stroke changes take a while to learn. The brain takes at least three weeks to develop and learn a new pattern. Therefore, work on your stroke every day and, in time, the most efficient stroke will become natural. For swimmers who can feel each part of their body during a stroke, changes may come quickly; but other swimmers, particularly beginning swimmers or those who have come from another sport, rely more heavily on external feedback than on how they feel in the water, so the process takes longer. Remember to be patient. Also, don't forget that everyone's stroke varies; just because you swim differently does not mean it is wrong for you. You will adapt to your own stroke.

Proper stroke mechanics should help you develop and maintain a rapid turnover without sacrificing efficiency for speed. Speed, efficiency, and endurance are essential for success in open water swimming, whether your swim is 1.5 miles or 30 miles. Next, in chapter 6, we'll apply these stroke training techniques to workouts specifically devised to fit your goals, your event, and your fitness level.

6

Training for Faster Swims

The decision to do a triathlon, an open water swim, or a series of each must come months, possibly a year or more, in advance of the event to ensure sufficient planning and training to succeed in the swim. Once you have decided to try swimming in open water or to compete in a triathlon, you need to determine which swim to attempt (see chapter 10), the distance to swim, and your goals for the swim. The swim needs to be feasible. If you have never swum, trying the Ironman with a 2.4-mile swim may not be feasible or recommended. You may need more training time to learn to swim more efficiently. For an open water swimmer who has only swum one to three miles, conquering Lake Tahoe, Loch Ness, or the Catalina or English Channels may not be feasible goals. Feasibility is based on numerous factors, such as your physical condition, athletic ability, available training time per day and before the event, financial resources, and mental stamina. You may think a goal is feasible, but as you train, you may find you are not improving quickly enough to be successful. This chapter will help you determine if your goal is feasible and how to train for it.

I was asked to train a 50-year-old to swim the Catalina Channel. He had the time and finances to train but didn't want to swim as far as I thought necessary to succeed. He was not mentally prepared to swim the long hours. In his first attempt,

91

he went into severe hypothermia within a few hundred yards of shore; he failed. He decided to try again, but I agreed to help him only if he did what I asked of him. He did and set the record for the oldest man to swim Catalina in under 11 hours.

DEVELOPING GOALS

Goals are the parameters within which your mind allows or pushes your body to perform. The higher you set your goals (within reason), the greater your chance for success. The more you ask of yourself, the more you will receive. A goal needs to be quantifiable and positive. It needs to be what you want to happen, not what you don't want to happen. Finally, goals need to be realistic but challenging.

A goal needs to be seasonal, since this helps you plan your training and keeps your focus throughout the season. You need to decide on a swim, triathlon, or a series of either. If you are a beginner and you have no idea of your ability but have a desire to do an open water swim or a triathlon, decide how much time

and money you want to invest and balance this assessment with your desire. If your goal is to compete in the Hawaiian Ironman and you are 50 years old, you may need many years to get in shape, to compete in numerous shorter triathlons, build up to an Ironman, and, finally, to qualify for the Hawaiian event. Achieving each part may take a year or more.

Divide your long-range goal into several smaller goals. For example, if you are shooting to compete in the Ironman, the first year you will get in shape for the three sports, compete in short races for one or more sports, and learn as much as possible. Go to a few triathlon clinics and watch a few events. Talk to competitors; you may find training partners, or maybe a swim, run, or bike club to train with. In the second year, you might compete in a few short triathlons and plan a taper for the last triathlon; keep researching, training, and learning about what you like or don't like in training and races. In the third year, you might compete in a few short triathlons and a few of the Ironman triathlons. You should learn a tremendous amount about yourself through the discipline needed to train and compete. If you qualify for the Hawaiian event, great; if not, keep working for that goal. For a person already in shape and 30 years younger, you can jump into one or a few triathlons your first year. If you like to train and compete, set higher goals the next year.

The first step toward achieving your goals is to write them down to make them more real. Quantify each goal by establishing both short- and long-term goals for practice and a race or a series of races. When you are establishing your goals, you need to know the difference between outcome-based and performance-based goals. Outcome-based goals relate to how you place; your goal compares the place you want to achieve against how you placed in previous performances. Performance-based goals compare the time you want to achieve to your times in past competitions (under similar conditions). Performance-based goals are better than outcome-based goals, because you can't control how anyone else trains or performs in a race, so other swimmers' performances should not affect how you think you did. You also can't control Mother Nature. Your time may be an hour slower than your goal for a triathlon, but in rough weather, you may actually have performed better.

As a more advanced swimmer or triathlete, you may be planning to compete in 6 to 12 races during the year. Determine which races you will compete in and the importance of each. If you are a triathlete, will the major triathlons be of Olympic or Ironman distance? If you are a triathlete, will you compete in many different triathlon distances? What is the order of the races and how will this affect training? For the professional open water swimmer, similar questions need to be asked. (How to train for a series of swims or triathlons is discussed later in this chapter, and chapter 10 provides contact information on specific races.)

After determining your goals and event, formulate an overall training plan to achieve success. The four components of a training plan are (1) elements of training (which include swim training, supplemental training, flexibility training, and nutrition); (2) intensity of training (which includes the four training categories: aerobic, endurance, anaerobic, and power); (3) planning the three season phases (early, main, and taper) and the schedules (yearly, monthly, weekly, and daily); and (4) evaluating training (overtraining, balancing training, training log, and rest).

Next, develop a yearly schedule to achieve your goals, and from this schedule, develop a weekly and daily plan. Your goals will guide how many practices you need to do a week (frequency), how many miles you need to swim (volume), and how long each workout must be (duration). You will learn how to develop each of these schedules in this chapter.

PURPOSE OF TRAINING

The purpose of training is to prepare for a specific swim or series of swims. There are six triathlon swimming distances: .24–.62 mile, .62–1.24 miles, .9 mile, 1.24–2.48 miles, and 2.4 miles and above. USA Triathlon, the governing body for the sport in the United States, hosts six national championships with distances of .1 mile, .5 mile, 1.2 miles, and 1.5 kilometers. The nationals include club, collegiate, distance, long course, sprint, and youth championship divisions. USS hosts four national championships in open water. The distances are the 3-mile, 5-mile, 10-mile, and 16-mile. International competitions have been held in the 16-mile. In 1996, the FINA committee added the 3-mile distance for the world championship. Also, there are international races ranging from 10 to 40 miles. Table 6.1 compares distances in yards, miles, meters, and kilometers.

Each swim distance requires a different training program. The frequency of training also depends on the distance to be swum,

TABLE 6.1

Distances, English and Metric

Yards	Miles	Meters	Kilometers
176	.1	161	.16
264	.15	241	.24
352	.2	352	.3
440	.25	402	.4
528	.3	483	.5
616	.35	563	.56
704	.4	644	.6
792	.45	724	.72
880	.5	805	.8
968	.55	885	.88
1,056	.6	966	.97
1,093	.621	1,000	1.00
1,144	.65	1,046	1.05
1,232	.7	1,127	1.1
1,320	.75	1,207	1.2
1,408	.8	1,288	1.3
1,496	.85	1,368	1.4
1,584	.9	1,449	1.45
1,672	.95	1,529	1.5
1,760	1.0	1,610	1.6
2,200	1.25	2,000	2
3,344	1.9	3,000	3
4,400	2.5	4,000	4
5,956	3.1	5,000	5
6,565	3.73	6,000	6
7,656	4.35	7,000	7
8,747	4.97	8,000	8
9,838	5.59	9,000	9
10,912	6.2	10,000	10
13,112	7.45	12,000	12
16,403	9.32	15,000	15
21,859	12.42	20,000	20
27,333	15.53	25,000	25
32,789	18.63	30,000	30
38,262	21.74	35,000	35
43,718	24.84	40,000	40
49,192	27.95	45,000	45
54,648	31.05	50,000	50

Note: 1 kilometer = 1,000 meters; 1 mile = 1,760 yards.
To convert: kilometers = miles $\times$ 1.61; miles = kilometers $\times$ .621.

as discussed in more detail below. If you are swimming a .5- to 2-mile event and are in good shape, you may only need to swim three times a week. If you are swimming 16 miles, you may need to swim six times a week for 2 to 6 hours a day. Suggested training for all triathlon and open water races is presented later in this chapter.

ELEMENTS OF TRAINING

There are four elements of training: swim training, supplemental training, flexibility training, and nutrition. Each is vital to achieving your goal. Each is detailed below.

Swim Training

Training in open water is obviously the most ideal situation to prepare for an open water race or event, but most athletes have to train in pools. Whether the race or swim event will occur in the ocean, a lake, or a river will determine the optimum training medium (figure 6.1). Ideally, the long training swim should occur in the same medium, but this is not always practical. If the event is a 21-mile ocean race, the ocean may be too cold during training in February for a 7-mile swim, or the swimmer may not be able to move to the ocean until the last month or two of training. In such cases, swimming the right training distance, whether it be in a pool or in the ocean, is more important than training in the same medium. So, if you only have access to a pool, by all means go there and swim the distance.

DRINKING FLUIDS FREQUENTLY

Keep in mind the importance of drinking fluids during practice (see chapter 9). Whether you are in the pool or in the open water, drink water every 15 minutes or between each set. On your weekly long swim, try to have someone swim or paddle the fluid out to you. Ideally, if a paddler can be with you throughout this swim each week, this support can help you physically and mentally. In any practice longer than two hours, make sure you drink carbohydrate fluid replacement in addition to water at these 15-minute intervals.

Figure 6.1 Lake at U.S. Swimming open water training camp in Colorado Springs.

Supplemental Training

Another component of effective training for your open water swim is supplemental training. You will need to include various types of supplemental training in your program. Depending on your time or personal preferences, these include weight training, circuit training, swimming-specific weight machines, calisthenics, running, and cycling. Supplemental training is important to develop overall conditioning, greater flexibility, and strength. It may also help to overcome weaknesses in the body due to injury, illness, or inactivity, and may prevent boredom in training.

Weight Training. The basic weight program outlined below details the types of exercises, the number of repetitions, and the procedure for increasing pounds and sets. For distance swimming, lower weights and higher repetitions are ideal, since this adds to aerobic and endurance training. Large, powerful muscles aren't needed for long-distance swimming and triathlons. There are also some general calisthenics that can help develop flexibility and strength and protect the muscles, joints, and tendons for specific muscles of the body. You can alternate calisthenics with the weight program to help stretch your muscles as you build them.

To incorporate the weight training exercises into your training program, first follow the detailed directions below and follow the directions on machines in the weight room. Also, if possible, find an expert to make sure you are lifting properly and to correct your technique, if necessary.

To determine what weight you can lift, test yourself on each machine with one repetition maximum. Start at a weight you can lift, add five pounds, and try lifting again. Continue adding weight in five-pound increments until you can't lift the weight. This is your maximum weight for that machine. Follow this procedure for each lift. Once you do this, begin your weight circuit program by lifting 60 percent of your maximum on each machine for the desired number of sets and reps. Over the weeks as you reach the maximum you can lift, drop the weight by 20 percent and add another set. Continue until you have reached three sets. This is the maximum number of sets you want to lift. Table 6.2 summarizes some guidelines for frequency and repetitions in weight training. Depending on the race distance for which you are training you may want to do more or fewer sets. A weight trainer should be able to assist you in developing a specific program.

The exercises listed below and the order in which you do them may be adjusted to the specific weight room you are using. It is beneficial to alternate leg and arm exercises or to break up the weight exercises with calisthenics.

Long triceps pull

Leg lifts on back—30 reps

Short triceps pull

Half press-ups—30 reps

Leg squats

Push-ups—15 reps

Single arm pulleys

Leg lifts on stomach—30 reps

Bench press

TABLE 6.2

Frequency and Repetitions

Week	Repetitions	Sets
1	6, 8, 10	1
2	8, 10, 12	1
3	10, 12, 14	1
4	6, 8, 10 (add 5 lbs.)	1
5	8, 10, 12	1
6	10, 12, 14	1
7	6, 8, 10 (add 5 lbs.)	1
8	8, 10, 12	1
9	10, 12, 14	1
10	6, 8, 10	2
11	8, 10, 12	2
12	10, 12, 14	2
13	6, 8, 10 (add 5 lbs.)	2
14	8, 10, 12 (add 5 lbs.)	2
15	10, 12, 14 (add 5 lbs.)	2
16	6, 8, 10 (add 5 lbs.)	2
17	8, 10, 12 (add 5 lbs.)	2
18	10, 12, 14	2
19	6, 8, 10	3
20	8, 10, 12	3
21	10, 12, 14	3
22	6, 8, 10 (add 5 lbs.)	3
23	8, 10, 12	3
24	10, 12, 14	3
25	6, 8, 10 (add 5 lbs.)	3
26	8, 10, 12 (add 5 lbs.)	3
27	10, 12, 14 (add 5 lbs.)	3

Sit-ups—50 to 150 reps

Leg raises—front

Leg raises—back

Wrist curls—front 10 reps

Wrist curls—back 10 reps

Wall slides—10 reps (10 sec. each)

Flutter kick—10 sec. to 2 min.

Double arm pulleys

Leg raises on side—20 reps

Full press-ups—30 reps

Swimming-Specific Weight Machines. In addition to the above exercises, there are two swimming-specific weight machines that can help improve your swimming. The first is the Simuswim 2000 (figure 6.2). This is a dryland bench that allows you to practice your stroke with resistance. The unique feature of this machine over the other brands on the market is that the bench moves, allowing you to rotate your body as you would in swimming. The second type of machine, Power Rack, is for in-the-water resistance training (figure 6.3). You are attached to the machine with a seat belt. When you push off the wall you swim as fast as you can for 15 feet. The machine provides resistance, challenging your ability to swim quickly. The number of pounds you use can be adjusted to your ability. This machine is made by Total Performance.

Calisthenics. Calisthenics are an important part of supplemental training. The most beneficial exercises include leg lifts, leg raises on side and back, flutter kick, half- and full-press-ups, and sit-

Figure 6.2 Simuswim 2000.

Figure 6.3 Power Rack.

ups. These help protect the back muscles through strengthening and stretching. Visit your local coach or trainer to help you with calisthenics exercises or refer to Bob Anderson's *Stretching*.

Cross Training. Running and cycling are good cross-training sports for swimming, especially early in the training plan, since these two sports develop general aerobic capacity and overall conditioning. In the early season, alternating these sports with swimming may help maintain your enthusiasm during the arduous process of getting into shape.

Flexibility Training

A flexibility program is designed to stretch the whole body. It is imperative to stretch before and after weights and before and after swimming to warm up your muscles and avoid injury. Further, your muscles will shorten as you lift weights or exercise a fair amount. This muscle shortening can lead to improper stroke mechanics. By stretching your muscles after weights or swimming, you can prevent this problem.

The following exercises make up a basic stretching program. Perform all exercises slowly, without bouncing, 5 to 10 times, holding each stretch for 6 to 10 seconds. Do each exercise three times daily in the order illustrated. Don't hold your breath while exercising. You should feel a comfortable pulling sensation but no discomfort. If you experience sharp or persistent pain while stretching, stop. The stretching program should take 15 to 20 minutes. Follow the techniques illustrated below. If one doesn't make sense, contact a local coach or teacher at a gym.

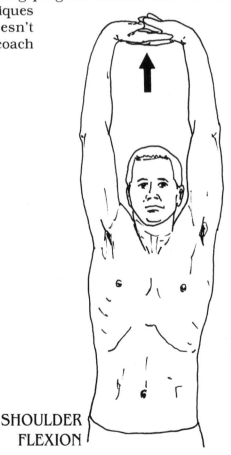

NECK FLEXION

SHOULDER
FLEXION

TOWEL STRETCH

POSTERIOR SHOULDER STRETCH

INFERIOR SHOULDER STRETCH

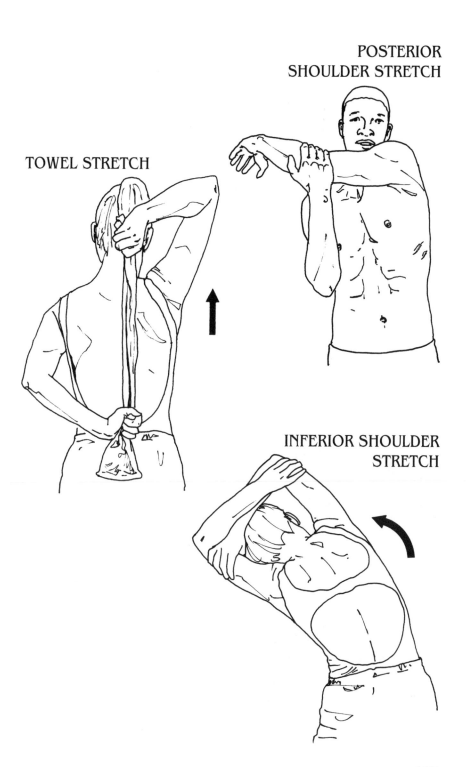

SHOULDER EXTENSION
STRETCH

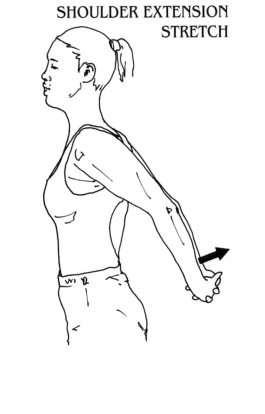

FULL-BODY STRETCH

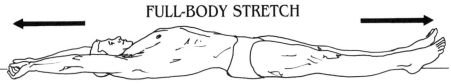

LOWER TRUNK
ROTATIONS

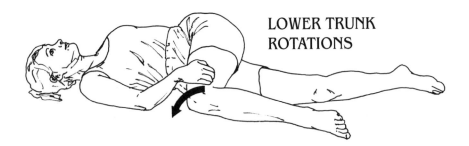

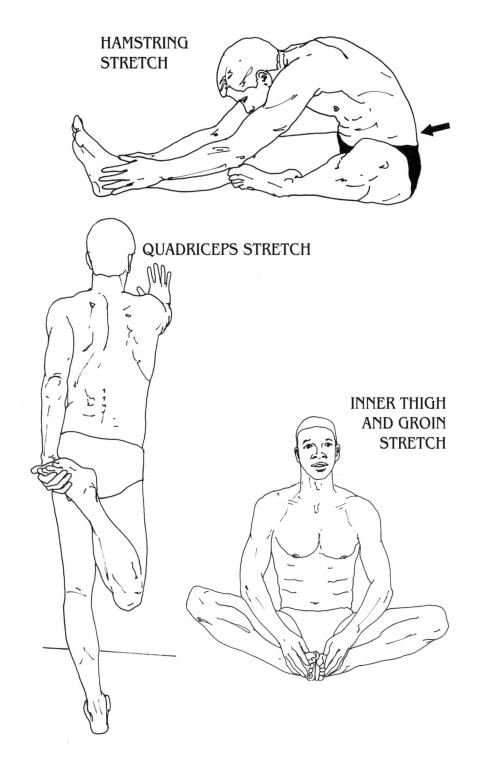

HAMSTRING
STRETCH

QUADRICEPS STRETCH

INNER THIGH
AND GROIN
STRETCH

MID-BACK STRETCH

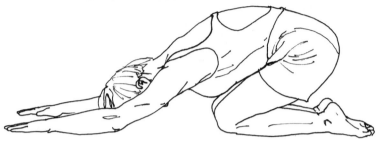

CALF STRETCH

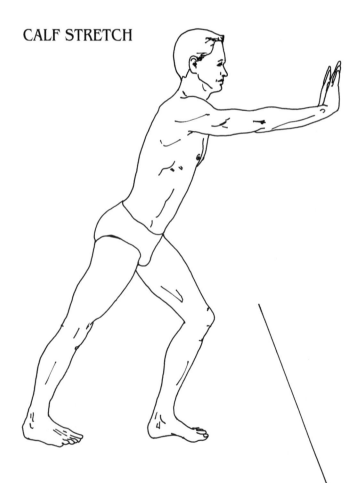

NUTRITION

Nourishment is very important for an open water swimmer and triathlete. From the first day of training until the swim is over, a well-balanced diet is essential. Eating needs to be consistent; eating correctly needs to become a habit.

Throughout the three training phases, eat three meals a day, consisting of meat or meat substitutes, milk and dairy products, grains, fruits, and vegetables. Drink at least eight glasses of water a day. Drink during every practice, preferably every 15 minutes. Take a multiple vitamin with iron daily. Most swimmers have an iron deficiency because of the stress training puts on their bodies.

It is important that you maintain a proper diet regimen to stay in the best condition possible. The body constantly needs carbohydrates, fats, proteins, vitamins, minerals, and water to perform at its best. These nutrients provide energy, maintain body tissue, and regulate the body processes. The body's daily intake should be 55 to 70 percent carbohydrate, 20 to 30 percent fat, and 10 to 18 percent protein.

Recently, a diet high in fat (over 50 percent fat) instead of carbohydrates has gained some popularity; however, the United States Surgeon General has indicated that a high-fat diet may not be beneficial and may be dangerous later in life. High-fat diets, being sold for a profit, have not been around long enough to evaluate their long-term effects. Medical opinion indicates a high-fat diet increases chances for heart disease. This also appears true of the high protein–low carbohydrate diet that is also popular right now.

The body's primary source of energy comes from carbohydrates and fats. Carbohydrates digest rapidly and provide quick and long-lasting energy. There are two kinds of carbohydrates: complex (starches) and simple (sugars). Fats protect the intestines, add a source of energy, and prevent the skin from becoming too dry and flaky. However, avoid too many saturated fats and simple sugars, better known as "junk food."

Protein is the second most abundant substance in the body. It builds new cells in the muscles, blood, bones, teeth, hair, and glands. Protein is a poor source of energy during exercise and should be complemented with carbohydrates and fats.

Energy can't come directly from vitamins, so massive doses will not help if you don't eat the correct foods. Vitamins do, however, help promote normal digestion and normal growth, and help the body resist infection. Similarly, minerals are essential for proper metabolism and aid in proper bone, teeth, and tissue growth. You should rely on the proper foods to supply your body with vitamins and minerals, not on supplements.

Water is the main component of cells, urine, perspiration, and blood. It is the by-product of every energy-producing chemical reaction in the body. Without a sufficient supply of water, muscles become weak, you tire easily, and toxic by-products build up in the bloodstream. Check your hydration level by weighing yourself regularly. Also, your urine should flow easily and not be dark and/or concentrated. If it does not flow easily or is concentrated, you need to drink more water.

If you decide to lose weight, never crash diet in the middle of training. Select a responsible plan, such as moderately reducing caloric intake, and planning to lose the weight over numerous months. To lose one pound of fat, you must burn 3500 calories. At mealtimes, stop eating as soon as the hunger pangs subside and drink extra water at each meal. Don't skip breakfast or any meal, since this makes you more hungry and may cause you to overeat at the next meal. Skipping meals will also have an adverse effect on training. If you don't eat between practices, your body will absorb its own muscle. Muscles need energy to work. If no fluid or food is supplied, the body will eat what is stored in it. The body will use muscle for energy before fat. Be sensible and eat between practices.

DO NOT MIX: ALCOHOL AND OPEN WATER

Be very cautious about using two things: alcohol and drugs. Alcohol tends to cause dehydration, which can be very dangerous during training, during a swim, or after a swim. It is illegal to use alcohol in any sanctioned swims, because it is an artificial aid. Beyond that, if you plan to celebrate after a swim, drink water and eat some food before you drink alcohol. The alcohol will affect you very quickly when you are fatigued. Further, if you have been in salt water, alcohol will burn your throat terribly, so be careful. It is also illegal on most swims for the navigator or crew to have alcohol. If people are drinking, it puts the swimmer and crew not only in danger but also liable for lawsuits if anyone is injured.

FINA and USA Triathlon rules include a long list of illegal drugs. Drugs may enhance performance, but in endurance events they can be deadly. Caffeine, taken in excess, is also illegal. Caffeine acts as a diuretic and can cause death on a long swim. Steroids are some of the most deadly drugs and have dangerous effects on the body, including causing tumors and sterility.

In some international swims and triathlons, drug testing is performed. There will be more as triathlons gain Olympic status and in all FINA open water swims in the future.

INTENSITY OF TRAINING

The training component involves how energy is produced, the three types of muscle fibers, the training categories, how to train each category, and the training itself. In order to produce energy to make the body perform there are two major types of energy production: anaerobic—without oxygen—and aerobic—with oxygen. Within the anaerobic systems there are two energy systems which produce energy. In the first, energy is produced for only 5 to 10 seconds. There is not a sprint swimming event, let alone a triathlon or open water swimming event, that is completed in such a small amount of time. In the second type, energy is produced for 10 seconds to 2 minutes. There are many swimming events that are completed in this amount of time, but no open water or triathlon events.

The aerobic system can supply energy almost indefinitely, as oxygen is continuously supplied to the muscles. In the muscles, the oxygen resynthesizes lactic acid into glucose, with the result of producing energy. In spite of the definition of "anaerobic" as "without oxygen," both the anaerobic and the aerobic systems use oxygen. After 15 seconds of swimming, oxygen is used to a small degree for energy production. After four minutes, this usage switches to over 50 percent oxygen. By 20 minutes, all energy is produced through the use of oxygen (table 6.3).

Lactate is produced when muscles are working. The body can be trained to tolerate this lactate production up to a point. However, once this point is reached, aerobic production has to take over, or the lactate level will prevent the muscles from

TABLE 6.3

Type of Energy Production Over Time			
Time	**Distance**	**% of anaerobic**	**% of aerobic**
0–10 sec.	15 yards	100	0
10–15 sec.	25 yards	80	20
2 min.	200 yards	60	40
4 min.	350 yards	50	50
10 min.	900 yards	30	70
20 min.	1,700 yards	22	78

performing. See Ernie Maglisco's *Swimming Even Faster* for a more in-depth explanation.

The human body has fast- and slow-twitch (white and red) muscle fibers. Each person's muscles have a preponderance of one or the other. However, a third fiber, type III, can be trained as either fast or slow. This is why a distance swimmer, after years of training, can become a great sprinter like Tom Jaeger, Tim Shaw, or Bill Babishoff. Each started as a distance swimmer, and later in their careers became internationally ranked sprinters. Thus, whether you have a preponderance of fast, slow, or type III muscle fibers, it is important to train each type of muscle fiber through various training categories.

There are four basic training categories that open water swimmers should include in their training program: aerobic, endurance, lactate or anaerobic, and power training. These training categories train each of the three types of muscle fibers.

Aerobic Training

Aerobic training is not very intense training. The higher your oxygen capacity, the better your aerobic capacity will be. Aerobic training increases aerobic capacity and allows you to perform longer. Long sets, lower training heart rate targets, and short rest develop aerobic capacity. Aerobic training should make up 20 to 30 percent of your training per week.

Endurance Training

Endurance is the ability to swim continuously in an efficient and effective manner for a number of miles or hours. Endurance is trained by long sets of high intensity (higher training heart rate targets than aerobic training) with short rest. The higher intensity level increases the aerobic capacity also. This type of training needs to be 60 to 70 percent of your training per week.

THE BENEFITS OF TRAINING PARTNERS

Many swimmers and triathletes train together, regardless of their gender. Ute Schafer of Germany, one of the top international triathletes, feels it is vitally important to be challenged by better competition in practice and therefore trains with men. Men also benefit from swimming with women, since women tend to train more consistently and usually at a higher intensity level than do men. Most pool swimmers swim with the opposite sex not only because it enhances the training level, but because the sport has been coed since it began. Almost all masters swimming teams throughout the U.S. are coed. In the marathon swims, men's and women's times are quite comparable.

Anaerobic or Lactate Training

As stated above, the anaerobic system usually supplies energy for a short period of time but can have effect for up to four minutes, after which the system can be depleted if the aerobic system doesn't kick in promptly. Anaerobic training involves short sets of high intensity with long rest. It is important to train the anaerobic system, since you may need to sprint at the beginning and end of a swim, hold your breath to go under waves, or swim faster in the middle of a race. This type of training needs to be 10 to 15 percent of your weekly training.

Power Training

Power training involves short sets at above-race pace with long rest. Power training conditions you to do a quick sprint when needed, usually for the start and finish of a race. Again, make sure you train at this energy level to improve your overall swimming capability. Power training should be included in 5 percent of your training each week.

TRAINING HEART RATE

The best way to determine your heart rate is to take your pulse on the inside of your wrist or on the carotid artery in your neck (see figure 6.4, *a* and *b*). Find your carotid by sliding your index and middle fingers across your neck from the Adam's apple to either the right or left until you feel your pulse. Take your pulse for a minute. The pulse should be between 40 and 70 beats per minute, but this rate depends on each individual, one's age, fitness level, and other factors.

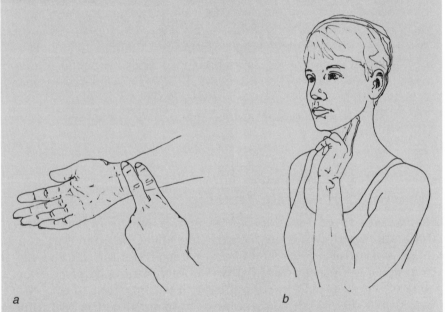

a   *b*

Figure 6.4 Take your pulse to determine your heart rate at (*a*) the inside of your wrist or (*b*) on the carotid artery in your neck.

To determine training intensities:

1. Take your heart rate for 60 seconds first thing in the morning = HR Resting _____

2. 220 – Age = HR Max _____

3. HR Max – HR Resting = HR Range

4. (HR Range × % Effort) + HR Resting = Training HR _____

Example

1. HR Resting = 60
2. 220 − 29 = 191   (HR Max)
3. 191 − 60 = 131   (HR Range)
4. (131 × .50) + 60 = 125.5 (Training HR at 50 % effort)

Now figure out your training heart rate for the percentages shown in table 6.4. If you are taking 10-second pulses, divide each Training HR by 6.

TABLE 6.4

Heart Rate Correlated to Percent Effort

Percent effort	Training heart rate	Pulse for 10 seconds
60%	_____	_____
70%	_____	_____
75%	_____	_____
80%	_____	_____
85%	_____	_____
88%	_____	_____
90%	_____	_____
93%	_____	_____
95%	_____	_____
98%	_____	_____
100%	_____	_____
110%	_____	_____

Table 6.5 shows a breakdown of the training categories—aerobic, endurance, and anaerobic. Included in this table is the percentage of the maximum heart rate needed to train each energy system of the body. The table allows for individual differences and the fact that every 10 years after age 25, your maximum heart rate will drop an average of 10 beats. The percentages of the maximum are vitally important, since if you swim at a higher or lower pulse rate, you may be training a different energy system. Therefore, it is essential to monitor your heart rate in training.

TABLE 6.5

The Body's Energy Systems

Name	% of heart rate	Purpose
Aerobic		
Recovery	60–70%	Warmup or recovery
Endurance		
Endurance 1	80%	Basic endurance; below anaerobic threshold; 300- to 5000-meter sets; rest 5 to 30 seconds.
Endurance 2	85%	Threshold endurance training; 100- to 3000-meter sets; rest 10 to 60 seconds.
Endurance 3	88%	Overload endurance training; 50- to 1000-meter sets; rest 30 seconds to 2 minutes.
Anaerobic		
Sprint 1	92%	Lactate tolerance; buffering, less acidosis; 90 to 93% of season's best; 100- to 800-meter sets; distances of 75 to 200 meters; rest 1 to 10 minutes.
Sprint 2	95%	Lactate production; 92 to 95% of season's best; 100- to 600-meter sets; distances of 25 to 75 meters; rest 1 to 5 minutes.
Sprint 3	Maximum 102%	Power training; 110% of season's best; 200- to 300-meter sets; distances of 10 to 35 meters; rest 30 seconds to 5 minutes.

In open water swimming, all swims, whether 1.5 or 21 miles, are distance events. Each relies primarily on aerobic capacity to generate energy. This implies the aerobic and endurance systems need to be emphasized in training, yet speed development is also essential. This means each system of the body needs to be trained (see table 6.5).

In the past eight years, such international pool swimmers as Australian Kieran Perkins, and Americans Chad Hundeby, Tobie Smith, and Amy Lindbloom have done better in pool competitions after having some success in open water swims, because each improved his or her aerobic capacity through long-distance swims and at the same time made sure not to sacrifice the speed element in training.

In 1948, Greta Anderson won the gold medal in the 100 freestyle and a silver in the 400 free relay in the London Olympics and made it to the finals in the 400 in the 1952 Helsinki Olympics. After emigrating to the United States, Greta began an open water marathon swimming career. Not only did she set numerous world records for women, but she also beat most of the men in these competitions. She set world records in the Salton Sea, the 18-mile Lake St. John, the 25-mile Atlantic City, a 42-mile double crossing of Catalina (this record lasted 19 years), and single crossings of the English Channel in both directions. Considering that her world record for the 100 freestyle set in 1949 lasted until 1956, her speed and endurance abilities were amazing. In addition to training in open water, Greta swam in the pool. She never neglected the speed aspect of her training.

Other great pool swimmers who switched to open water are John Kinsella, Florence Chadwick, and Gertrude Ederle. John Kinsella won a silver medal in the 1500 meters in the 1968 Olympics and a gold in a relay in the 1972 Olympics. He then set every major open water record except the English Channel from 1975 through 1979. Florence Chadwick had placed 2nd in the nationals early in her career and fourth at the 1936 Olympic trials in the backstroke. She went on to set world records for the English and Catalina Channels and many other less-known swims besides. The most famous of these converts, Gertrude Ederle, set nine world records in the pool, won three Olympic medals, and became the first woman to swim the English Channel in 1926 in 14 hours and 39 minutes. Gertrude held the world record for women until 1950, when Florence Chadwick broke it.

PLANNING YOUR TRAINING PROGRAM

When planning your training program, make sure to train the aerobic and anaerobic systems throughout the program. Divide your program plan into three phases: early season, main season, and taper. Then develop your yearly, monthly, weekly, and daily schedules.

Your Seasonal Plan

Planning your training for an entire season starts by determining how much time you have and need to prepare for the event. Counting from the event backwards, the ideal length of your training depends mainly on the distance to be swum. If the swim is only 2.4 miles, a few months of training are sufficient in most cases. The conditions of the swim also play a part. Let's say, however, the 2.4-mile swim is across the San Francisco Bay in January, where the water temperature is 48 to 51 degrees. Up to a year of preparation might be necessary to acclimatize to the cold water.

In devising a seasonal training schedule, first break the preparation period into three phases: early season, main season, and taper. Then develop a yearly, monthly, weekly, and daily schedule based on the seasonal schedule. The sample schedules presented later in this chapter delineate the three training phases.

Seasonal Swim Training. In the seasonal schedule, plan the distance of one straight practice swim per month, working from the approximate swim date backwards. I have designed a sample plan for each triathlon distance, each USS open water distance, and the major channel swims. Each plan can be adjusted to fit the swimmer and distance of the swim. Each month, regardless of which training phase, swim one straight practice swim of the mileage listed in table 6.6 under race conditions. Use the same breaks, the exact food, and signals as you would in a race (see chapter 9).

The distance of these practice swims gradually increases and reaches a peak about 10 days prior to the event. For an event over six miles, you need not train more than 80 percent of the total swim mileage unless you feel it is necessary for your mental satisfaction.

Seasonal Supplemental Training Plan. When you devise a seasonal plan for your supplemental training, plan to conclude most of the supplemental training after the main phase of the season. For example, with a swim planned for late August, an 11-month supplemental training plan can be divided as in tables 6.7, 6.8, and 6.9.

The early season typically includes the first 3 months of training for an 11-month training period. For open water swimming in the U.S., the early season is usually the months of October, November, and December. Limit the volume of swimming during

TABLE 6.6

Distance of Monthly Long Swim

#	Race length Month	.5 mi.	1 mi.	1.5 mi.	2.4 mi.	3 mi.	5 mi.	10 mi.	16 mi.	21 mi.
1	October	.22	.3	.35	.4	.5	.75	1.5	2	3
2	November	.24	.35	.4	.8	1	1	2.5	3	4
3	December	.26	.42	.5	1	1.25	1.5	3	4	5
4	January	.28	.47	.6	1.2	1.5	2	4	5	6
5	February	.3	.5	.75	1.5	1.75	2.5	5	6	7
6	March	.34	.6	.9	1.75	2	3	6	7	8
7	April	.38	.7	1	1.9	2.25	3.5	7	8	9
8	May	.42	.8	1.1	2.1	2.5	4	7.5	9	10
9	June	.46	.9	1.3	2.25	2.75	4.5	8	11	12
10	July	.5	1	1.5	2.4	3	5	8.5	13	14
11	August	Swim	Swim	Swim	Swim	Swim	Swim	Swim	Swim	17
12	September									Swim

TABLE 6.7

	.5 to 3 miles	5 to 10 miles	16 to 21 miles
Early Season Training Frequency			
1. Weights	2 times a week	3 times a week	3 times a week
2. Run and bike	3 times a week	3 times a week	3 times a week
3. Stretch	5 times a week	5 times a week	5 times a week
4. Swim	3 times a week	3 times a week	4 times a week

this phase and emphasize strength development and conditioning through other means. By incorporating nonswimming activities into your training during this stage, you can also prevent boredom or burnout later in the season. Stretching, weights, and running or biking are the most advantageous supplemental activities to swimming. Needless to say, the triathlete is doing sufficient supplemental training with running and biking, but lifting weights and stretching regularly are also important for preventing injury.

The main phase of the season encompasses the bulk of the training. Continuing the example from above, for open water swimming, the months of January until the middle of August comprise the main phase of the season. As training progresses, drop the run/bike portion and increase swimming to six times a week for most distances. Maintain weight training until three months before the swim. Continue stretching throughout the training period to help warm up your body, relieve soreness, and lessen the chances for injuries. An example of a main phase supplemental training plan for all distances is detailed in table 6.8. The taper phase is a two- to three-week period in August. An example of a taper supplemental training plan is detailed in table 6.9.

TABLE 6.8

Main Season Training Frequency	
1. Weights	3 times a week
2. Stretch	6 times a week
3. Swim	6 times a week

TABLE 6.9

Taper Training Frequency	
1. Swim	6 times a week
2. Stretch	6 times a week

Monthly, Weekly, and Daily Schedules

The monthly schedule simply breaks the yearly schedule into weeks (see table 6.10). Again, the long straight swims are listed and bolded. A smaller straight swim should occur each week of each month after the early season training period ends. These smaller swims don't have to be done in open water or race conditions until the last two months. However, doing them in open water under race conditions will help. Some months may have more or less full weeks, but this is immaterial. The planning begins from the swim backwards.

Alternate-Day Training. In each of the three training phases, an alternate-day training regime ensures that each training category will be trained. For example, an alternate-day training plan could involve longer training mileage and sets (endurance and aerobic) on Monday, Wednesday, Friday, and Saturday, and shorter mileage and challenging speed sets (anaerobic and power) on Tuesday and Thursday. Swimming the same mileage every day is fine, but your body and mind may react better to the variety of alternate-day training.

Use a pattern of training to build endurance and speed over the season. The best way to develop speed is through fast, short, repetitious sets (anaerobic and power). This practice can be accomplished in the pool or in open water. For example, in January or the first month of the main season, in the pool a speed set may be a set of 8 × 100 yards leaving on 3:30, swimming them as fast as possible, or in the open water swimming 100 strokes as fast as possible and 300 strokes easy for 6 repetitions. By May, you should have built up enough endurance through multiple training sessions to complete 2 to 3 sets of 6 × 100 yards and a similar improvement in open water. This is the training effect; it leads to muscle adaptation, improvement in aerobic capacity, and lactate tolerance.

Another way to practice swimming fast and at the planned stroke count for a swim is to use a Power Reel (figure 6.5). This

TABLE 6.10

Monthly Schedule by Weeks

Month	Week	.5 mi.	1 mi.	1.5 mi.	2.4 mi.	3 mi.	5 mi.	10 mi.	16 mi.	21 mi.
Oct.	1	.18	.2	.23	.25	.3	.5	1.2	1.5	2
	2	.2	.25	.28	.3	.4	.65	1.4	1.8	2.3
	3	.15	.18	.225	.2	.275	.4	1	1.2	1.8
	4	**.22**	**.3**	**.35**	**.4**	**.5**	**.75**	**1.5**	**2**	**3**
Nov.	1	.2	.25	.28	.5	.65	.8	2.1	2.25	2.5
	2	.22	.3	.35	.7	.85	.9	2.4	2.75	3.5
	3	.18	.23	.25	.6	.5	.7	1.8	1.9	2
	4	**.24**	**.35**	**.4**	**.8**	**1**	**1**	**2.5**	**3**	**4**
Dec.	1	.22	.3	.35	.75	1.1	1.2	2.7	3.25	3.5
	2	.24	.35	.4	.9	1.2	1.4	2.85	3.5	4
	3	.2	.28	.33	.7	.9	.9	2.4	2.8	3
	4	**.26**	**.42**	**.5**	**1**	**1.25**	**1.5**	**3**	**4**	**5**
Jan.	1	.24	.4	.45	1	1.3	1.7	3.25	3.75	4
	2	.26	.42	.5	1.1	1.4	1.85	3.75	4.5	5
	3	.22	.38	.4	.9	1.2	1.4	2.9	3	3.5
	4	**.28**	**.47**	**.6**	**1.2**	**1.5**	**2**	**4**	**5**	**6**
Feb.	1	.26	.43	.5	1.2	1.5	2.2	4	5	5
	2	.28	.45	.6	1.3	1.6	2.4	4.75	5.5	6
	3	.24	.4	.48	1.1	1.4	1.9	3.5	4	4
	4	**.3**	**.5**	**.75**	**1.5**	**1.75**	**2.5**	**5**	**6**	**7**
Mar.	1	.28	.48	.7	1.5	1.8	2.6	4.85	5	6
	2	.3	.5	.8	1.6	1.9	2.85	5.75	6.5	7
	3	.26	.45	.75	1.3	1.6	2.3	4.25	4.5	5
	4	**.34**	**.6**	**.9**	**1.75**	**2**	**3**	**6**	**7**	**8**

Month	Week									
Apr.	1	.32	.58	.75	1.6	2.1	3.1	5.3	5.5	7
	2	.34	.6	.9	1.7	2.15	3.4	6.7	7	8
	3	.3	.55	.8	1.4	1.9	2.9	4.5	5	6.5
	4	**.38**	**.7**	**1**	**1.9**	**2.25**	**3.5**	**7**	**8**	**9**
May	1	.36	.68	.8	1.75	2.3	3.6	6	6.5	7.5
	2	.38	.7	1	1.9	2.4	3.8	7.1	8	9
	3	.34	.65	.95	1.5	2.1	3.2	5	5.25	6
	4	**.42**	**.8**	**1.1**	**2.1**	**2.5**	**4**	**7.5**	**9**	**10**
June	1	.4	.78	.9	1.8	2.4	4.1	7	8	9
	2	.42	.8	1.1	2	2.6	4.3	7.75	9	10
	3	.38	.75	1	1.6	2.3	3.7	6	7	8.5
	4	**.46**	**.9**	**1.3**	**2.25**	**2.75**	**4.5**	**8**	**11**	**12**
July	1	.44	.88	1.2	2	2.6	4.6	7	9	10
	2	.46	.9	1.1	2.1	2.8	4.8	8.25	11	12
	3	.42	.85	1.3	1.9	2.5	3.9	6	8	9
	4	**.5**	**1**	**1.5**	**2.4**	**3**	**5**	**8.5**	**13**	**15**
Aug.	1	.4	.9	1.4	2.3	2.8	4.5	8	12	10
	2	T	T	T	T	T	T	T	T	12
	3	.25	.5	.8	1.2	1.5	2.4	4	6.5	13
	4	Swim	Swim	Swim	Swim	Swim	Swim	Swim	Swim	17
Sept.	1									10
	2									T
	3									7
	4									Swim

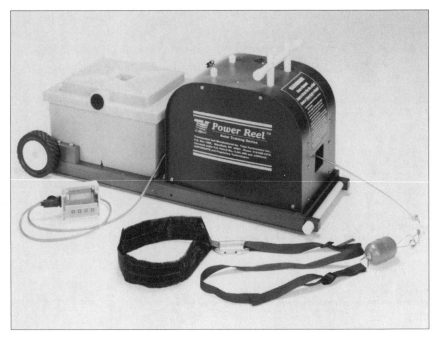

Figure 6.5   The Power Reel, the new power assistance machine.

machine pulls you at the desired speed across the pool and allows you to practice at race pace throughout all three training phases. In the early season, you probably won't be able to train at race pace and stroke count, whereas in the main phase, you may be slower because of the volume of training. Most people only swim at race pace during the taper. One of the problems with open water swimmers and triathletes is the tremendous volume of training, which affects speed. This revolutionary machine, developed by Total Performance, eliminates this problem of swimming slower, since you are able to swim at race pace during any of the training phases. Also, if you want to be able to maintain a certain stroke count but have never experienced swimming this stroke count, this machine can pull you at that speed to allow you to feel the desired stroke count and speed. Use the Power Reel two to three times a week throughout each training phase. After warm up and a short set, get on the machine. Before a long set, use the machine to remind you of the pace you want to hold and to help you train at a higher level. Do four to ten 25-meter repetitions. Have your coach watch for stroke errors and correct them immediately. Use the machine again after any stroke corrections.

To build endurance, straight swims at one pace are important. The swim may be four miles in the pool or in open water. You need to do one to two major swims a week, depending on the length of the swim, at the end of the season. Also, on Monday and Friday, swim shorter distance sets, such as 800, 1000, 1500, 2000, 3000, and 5000 yards in the pool or .5- to 5.0-mile repeats in open water.

An ideal training regime for each training phase is a combination of endurance and speed work in each practice, especially for swimmers or triathletes who may swim less than four practices a week. For example, if your ocean workout is six miles, the first four miles may be at one pace, while during the fifth and sixth miles you alternate 100 strokes fast and 100 easy. Similarly, in the pool workout, you may do sets of straight miles and sets of 50s, 100s, and 200s. In the workouts presented later in the chapter, for a 2.4- and a 16-mile swim (tables 6.11 and 6.12), the speed and endurance elements are evident. The 2.4-mile training assumes that the triathlete is training four days a week. Due to this regime, both endurance and speed are trained each day; however, endurance is emphasized on two of the days and speed is emphasized on the other two days. For the 16-mile swim, you should be training six days a week. Tuesday and Thursday practices are shorter and speed is emphasized. On the other four days, Monday and Friday are endurance repeats and some speed work, and Wednesday and Saturday are longer distance or, preferably, a straight swim. It is important to acclimatize not only your body but also your mind. As the distance of the swim increases, the mental component of the swim increases significantly. As discussed in more detail in chapter 7, the longer your head is in the water without much other human communication, the harder the practice and swim become.

Since triathletes are doing so much other training which will help with endurance, they need only swim three to four days a week. Triathletes who are excellent swimmers should swim two days a week in the early season, three days a week in the main season, and two days a week during the taper.

During the main phase of the training season, try to increase the mileage weekly. Your weekly distance may range from .5 to 8 miles, depending on the event you are training for. The increase should be 5 to 15 percent a week. (This is detailed later in this chapter.)

DON'T FORGET TECHNIQUE

One idea to work technique training into your everyday practices is to concentrate on your stroke on every odd length in a pool or at every odd mile in the open water. To figure your mileage in open water, ask a lifeguard the distance between towers, measure the course yourself in a car, if possible, or go by time. If you are a fast swimmer, gauge every 20 minutes as one mile, whether it is a warm up, easy swim, or fast swim. If you are a medium-skilled swimmer, use 25 minutes, and if you are a slow swimmer, use 30 minutes or more. If, however, you have no idea, swim a one-mile race in a measured course and use this time.

Taper Phase. Generally, a 10- to 14-day taper, beginning from the longest practice, works well. This gives your body sufficient time to recover and rest for the upcoming swim. Also, the taper helps you mentally prepare, since the long practice swim instills the needed confidence to conquer the upcoming swim. Typically, however, a female should begin tapering between 8 and 12 days prior to the event, a few more days if she is tall and muscular. For a 16-mile swim, the 10-day taper seems to work the best, but tapers depend on the individual. A taper for a male ranges from 11 to 21 days, more if he is a larger male or needs more rest. (A large or older swimmer, whether a man or a woman, needs extra rest.) Generally, a shorter swim may mean a shorter taper, while a longer swim may need a longer taper. It may take several years to figure out what taper works best for you for each distance.

Within the 10-day taper, the mileage gradually drops to the day of the swim. The goal of the last week of practice is to warm up thoroughly and gradually increase speed in each swim in order to feel good and strong. Do not overdo it.

If you are racing in a series of swims or triathlons, the amount of rest for each depends on the time between each race. For the open water professional circuit and the shorter open water swims, there are races every weekend from July through August. If one swim is the finale, as Atlantic City is for the open water professionals, this is the ideal time to concentrate on a full taper. It is important, however, to rest the day before a race in the six- to eight-week circuit. This period would entail just a short warm-up swim with little exertion.

For the triathlon season, which lasts longer but with races more evenly spread over time, there can be many mini-tapers with a larger taper before the finale. A mini-taper would be a two- to five-day reduction in training intensity and a slight reduction in the volume of training; the shorter amount for a short triathlon and the longer amount for a longer triathlon. This mini-taper will allow you to rest but keep the volume consistent for success at each triathlon throughout the series. You should swim, bike, and run a small amount the last two days. If you are recovering from an injury, a day of rest three days out will be beneficial. This still provides two days of easy training to prepare for the race.

Sample Training Plans. The weekly and daily schedules can be combined once the monthly breakdown has been completed. Tables 6.11 and 6.12 are two sample schedules used by two former athletes. Table 6.11 is the schedule for a 2.4-mile swim in the main training phase. This athlete was able to swim in a lake one day a week and in a pool three days a week. The sample schedule in Table 6.12 is for a 16-mile swim in the last month of training. This athlete was able to swim in the ocean three days a week—Monday, Wednesday, and Saturday—and in a pool the other three days.

PRACTICE TERMINOLOGY

To write practice schedules, use certain terms and abbreviations. The commonly used ones are defined here. For example, easy/fast (e/f) means that you will swim a certain distance at an easy speed followed by a certain distance at a fast speed. Negative split (ns) means swimming the first half of a repeat at a controlled speed and swimming the second half faster than the first. Building up (bu) or descending (d) a set means each repeat gets faster as the set progresses. Warm up (wu), loosen down (ld), kick (k), pull (p), and with (w/) so many seconds rest are the most common abbreviations used when writing a practice schedule. A *set* is a swim set unless noted as *k* or *p* sets.

TABLE 6.11

Example 1: Training for a 2.4-Mile Swim in June

Date	Day	Miles	Training
1	Monday	1.6	wu .3; 3 × 500 w/1:30; 300 bu k; 300 ld.
2		off	
3		1.4	wu .2; 800 bu; 6 × 100 k w/:10; 8 × 50 w/:10; 200 ld.
4		.7	wu .2; 8 × 75 w/1:15.
5		off	
6		1.8	Lake swim—wu .5, sprint 1 mile, .3 ld.
7		off	
8	Monday	1.8	wu .3; 3 × 600 d 1-3 w/:20; 200 k; 300 ld.
9		off	
10		1.6	wu. 3; 2 × 1000 w/:30; 100 ld.
11		.8	wu .2; 10 × 50 w/:45.
12		off	
13		2	Lake swim—wu .4, sprint 1.4 miles, .2 ld.
14		off	
15	Monday	1.9	wu .2; 5 × 400 d 1-3, 4-5 w/1:15; 6 × 50 k w/:10; 200 ld.
16		off	
17		1.7	wu .3; 2,000 e/f by 200; 200 ld.
18		.9	wu .2; 6 × 100 w/1:30; 100 ld.
19		off	
20		1.6	Lake swim—wu .2, sprint 1.4 miles
21		off	
22	Monday	2	wu 200; 8 × 250 w/:15 d 1-4, 5-8; 400 k; 200 ld.
23		off	
24		1.8	wu 200; 2 × 800 w/:30 d 1-2; 300 k; 12 × 25 k w/:15; 200 ld.
25		1	wu 300; 3 × (6 × 50) w/:40 1 set p, 1 set drill; 300 k; 100 fast; 200 ld.
26		off	
27		2.25	Lake swim—wu .25, sprint 1.8, .2 ld.
28		off	
29	Monday	2.1	wu .3; 300 in drills; 1000 bu; 4 × 75 k w/:15; 200 ld.
30		off	

TABLE 6.12

Example 2: Training for a 16-Mile Swim, the Taper

Date	Day	Miles	Training
1	Monday	11	wu .8; 4 × 2.4 miles d 1-2, 3-4 w/1; 200 k; 400 ld.
2		6.5	wu 1000, 600 k, 600 p; 12 × 300 d 1-3, w/:30; 12 × 100 k w/:15; 1600 p, e/f by 200; 300 fast; 800 ld.
3		9.5	wu 1; 3 miles e/f by .5; 2-mile sprint; 3 miles d 1-3; .4 k; .6 ld.
4		4.5	wu 1500; 6 × 50 w/:15; 3 × (8 × 100 w/ :40) w/1 d 1-8; 1000 bu k; 3 × 600 p.
5		7	wu 600, 600 k, 600 p; 4 × (5 × 200 w/ :40) w/1; 3 × 500 k w/:45; 1000, 500, 400, 300, 200, 100 p w/1; 1000 drill; 12 × 75 w/:15, d 1-4; 800 ld.
6		13	wu 1; 10 miles: d 1-4, 5-8, 9 easy, sprint 10; 1 mile e/f by 100 strokes;1 ld.
7		off	
8	Monday	11.5	wu 1; 3 × 3 miles: e/f by 1 mile, bu 4-6, 7-9 sprint, easy, sprint; 1 mile easy; .5 ld.
9		6	wu 1000, 500 k, 300 p; 4 × (6 × 75 w/:30) w/1; 10 × 200 k w/:20; 3 × 1000 p d 1-3; 2 × 400 e/f by 100 w/1; 400 ld.
10		10	wu 1; 4 miles bu; 3 miles d 1-3; 2 miles 1 easy, 1 fast.
11		5	wu 800, 500 k, 500 p; 20 × 25 w/:10; 4 × 400 w/:45 d 1-4; 3 × 600 k w/1; 2000 p; 20 × 25 w/:20 d 1-5; 600 ld.
12		7	wu 1000, 600 k, 400 p; 4 × 1000 bu 1-2, 3-4 w/1; 6 × 300 k w/:30; 8 × 300 p e/f by 150 w/:40; 10 × 100 w/1 d 1-3; 1000 ld.
13		12	wu 1; 9 miles: 6 @ 90%, 2 @ 60%, 1 @ 100%; 1 mile bu; 1 ld.
14		off	
15	Monday	10	wu 1; 2 × 4 miles: e/f by .5; 1 ld.
16		4	wu 1000, 400 k, 400 p; 4 × (4 × 50 w/:30) w/1; 2 × 800 k w/1:30; 4 × 500 p e/f by 100 w/:15; 2 × 250 w/1 d 1-2; 500 ld.

(continued)

TABLE 6.12 *(continued)*

Date	Day	Miles	Training
17		9	wu 1; 5 miles sprint; 2 miles working stroke; 1 ld.
18		5	wu 800, 500 k, 500 p; 12 × 50 w/:10; 3 × 600 w/1; 24 × 75 k w/:20; 1500 p bu; 6 × 150 drill w/:10; 600 ld.
19		7	wu 1000, 600 k, 400 p; 1000, 900, 800, 700, 600, 500, 400, 300, 200, 100 bu w/1; 5 × 400 k w/1; 6 × 250 p w/40; 20 × 50 d 1-5 w/:15; 500 ld.
20		11	wu 1; 8 miles: pace @ 85%; 1 mile drill; 1 ld.
21		off	
22	Monday	9	wu 1; 2 × 3.5 miles: e/f by 200 strokes w/1; .5 drill; .5 ld.
23		8	wu 1000, 900 k, 900 p; 2000 bu; 16 × 150 w/:30 bu; 40 × 50 k w/:10; 8 × 400 p e/f by 200 w/:30; 5 × 200 drill w/1; 1000 ld.
24		6.5	wu 1; 5 miles pace @ 90%; .5 ld.
25		6	wu 1000, 500 k, 300 p; 10 × 50 w/:10; 5 × 500 w/1 d 1-3, 4-5; 8 × 250 k w/:40 d 1-4, 5-8; 3000 p bu; 4 × 125 w/:50; 600 ld.
26		5	wu .4; 4 miles e/f by .5; .3 k; .3 ld.
27		4	wu .5; 3 miles bu to 90%; .3 drill, push k; .2 ld.
28		2.5	wu.5, 2 miles 85%.
29	Monday	1	1 mile 80%.
30		Warmup	
31		Swim	

For example, let's say that your daily practice schedule for the 15th day of training for the 2.4-mile swim calls for a 1.9-mile workout in the pool. The first workout can be written as follows: wu .2; 5 × 400 d 1-3, 4-5 w/1:15; 6 × 50 k w/:10; 200 ld. This shorthand means that once you enter the water, you swim .2 of a mile or 350 yards easy, concentrating on your stroke throughout. Next, you swim five 400s. The set requires you to descend (d), or get faster, from number one to number three and number four to number 5. To do this, you can concentrate on stroke on the first repeat, try to give 85 percent on the second repeat, and sprint the third repeat. The fourth repeat is easy, concentrating on stroke, while the fifth is a sprint, again thinking about stroke since you are tired. Between repeats, you rest one minute and 15 seconds. Next there is a set of six 50s of kicking (k) with or without a board. (If you have shoulder problems, don't use a kick board.) The rest between each repeat is 10 seconds. Finally, you loosen down (ld) 200 yards easy, stretching on each stroke.

The second workout example is on the 6th day of training and is a 13-mile practice. It involves a wu 1; 10 miles: d 1-4, 5-8, 9 easy, sprint 10; 1 mile e/f by 100 strokes; 1 ld. The first mile, you warm up (wu) and concentrate on your stroke. The main part of the practice is a 10-mile swim. This is broken into four parts. The first involves swimming four miles, starting easily and thinking about the stroke. On the second mile, you increase your speed to 80 to 85 percent of your fastest. You still concentrate on your stroke but maintain an even pace throughout the mile. In the third mile, you increase your speed to 90 percent. You need to press harder with your arms throughout the stroke. As you tire, concentrate on your follow through to maintain power in the stroke. In the fourth mile, you need to sprint. You have to increase your speed to 100 percent. You should push yourself, and all the muscles of your arms and legs should be burning. After a short break and fluid, repeat the first four miles the same way. On the ninth mile, you swim easily. You should use this mile to recover from the first eight and to prepare for the tenth mile. After a few minutes' rest, sprint mile 10. Concentrate on your legs and push yourself faster than on any other mile. Next, for mile 12, swim 100 strokes easy followed by 100 strokes fast (e/f). Repeat this pattern until the mile is over. It will be challenging to switch from easy to fast, but this is good practice for reacting to another swimmer making a move in a race. Finally, swim mile 13 easily and smoothly. Concentrate on your stroke and don't put any effort into the final mile.

Below is a discussion of an individual swim or triathlon and then the adaptation for a series of swims or triathlons. The basic training is the same. There are just some changes for extra rest between major competitions and for competing in more than one race. In addition, the months of early phase, main phase, and taper phase of the season may change, but the training doesn't.

PLANNING FOR OPEN WATER SERIES OF RACES

Your mileage plan for the year, month, and week is similar, until the taper phase, whether you are planning to do 1 race or 10 in a season. For example, if you are an open water swimmer, your training would begin in September with a short early-season period (September through October). Your main preparation period would be from November through mid to late June. You would then have a partial taper for a week to prepare for the first of six to eight races occurring in July and August, with competitions on Saturday or Sunday. Plan the partial taper to end a week before your first swim. Limit your volume from the partial taper through the series of races for the next six weeks (July 1 through the second week of August). Since you will be racing a long swim each week, you only need one other medium swim in the week, preferably on Tuesday. On the other days, you should swim half of this distance on Monday, Wednesday, and Thursday. Friday's mileage should be shorter.

For example, in the second week of July, the main swim is seven miles. If the race is on Saturday, Sunday is a rest day. Monday is a 3.5-mile swim, mainly working on recovery from the race. Tuesday's volume is 7 miles, with over 75 percent dedicated to endurance and the rest to speed. Wednesday's volume is 3.5 miles, emphasizing speed. Thursday's 3.5 miles is divided into endurance and speed work. Finally, Friday, if you feel good, do a comfortable 2.5 mile swim, or simply a 1-mile warm-up swim if you don't feel good.

Prior to the last race of the racing circuit, you should use a full taper to help recover from weekly marathons and to rest prior to the final swim in the series. Table 6.13 shows a sample schedule of the long swim each week for the open water series from mid June through the end of the series. The earlier training follows the 21-mile schedule in table 6.10. This is the training adjustment. Table 6.14 shows a sample daily training schedule for the same period. Again, adjust these schedules to your own physical and mental abilities.

PLANNING FOR TRIATHLONS

For the triathlon series, the races last most of the year. As a triathlete, you have two ways to handle the swimming training.

TABLE 6.13

Long Training Swim for Open Water Series

Month	Week	Miles
June	1	12
	2	9
	3	15
	4	8
July	1	7
	2	7
	3	6.5
	4	6.5
August	1	6
	2	5 (taper two weeks before last race)
	3	4
	4	3 (final swim)

TABLE 6.14

Daily Schedule

	Week								
Day	1	2	3	4	5	6	7	8	9
Sunday	—	—	—	—	—	—	—	—	—
Monday	4	3.5	3.5	3.25	3	3	2.5	3	2
Tuesday	8	7	7	6.5	6.5	6	5	4	3
Wednesday	4	3.5	3.5	3.25	3	3	2.5	3	1.5
Thursday	4	3.5	3.5	3.25	3	3	2.5	2.25	1.5
Friday	3.5	2.5	2.5	2.25	2	2	1.5	1.5	1
Saturday	8	R	R	R	R	R	R	R	R

You can plan for one major race and use the above training, or you can treat each race equally. For the latter choice, use the 11-month plan presented in table 6.10, and do the activities over 11 weeks, since the preparation period is shorter and there are more competitions throughout the year. This plan allows you to gradually increase the mileage for the major swims but in a shorter training period. Since none of the distances, except in the ultra triathlons, are over 2.4 miles, this plan is feasible. The longest ultra is 6 miles, so the 5- or 10-mile training could be adapted to 11 weeks also. If you have more than 11 weeks to prepare prior to the first race, you can expand the plan. The beginning weeks of mileage aren't very taxing, and the first two months could be done in a week if you are in shape and an experienced triathlete. The main component is planning. The volume of training is the same, but the frequency of training would increase weekly.

During the series of races, maintain the mileage, using one long swim and two to three shorter swim practices a week. On the long day, emphasize endurance training. On the other days, combine endurance and speed work. For example, for a swim distance of 2.4 miles, the long swim should be 2 miles, while the other days should be 1.5 miles. Use table 6.15 as a guide.

TABLE 6.15

TRAINING DISTANCES FOR TRIATHLON SERIES

	.5	1	1.5	2.4	5
Long day	.42	.8	1.1	2	4
Short day	.35	.6	.75	1.5	3

Again, you have to adjust the swims according to how you feel and the effects you have from the last race. If you need more rest before the race, reduce the volume or intensity of your last short practice.

EVALUATING YOUR TRAINING

Training for an open water swim or a triathlon is an arduous task that requires close monitoring to be successful and to help prevent injury or illness. Start your training off right by having a complete physical as a safety precaution before you start training. Once you have a clean bill of health, you can begin your training gradually. It is important to recognize the physiological changes that occur with training and overtraining.

Recognizing Overtraining

Positive changes which occur with training are muscle development, excellent cardiovascular development, amazing endurance, and usually a great tan. However, training can take its toll if it is not balanced with enough recovery time.

One good way to monitor your health and the tolls of training is to take your resting heart rate every morning before you get up. If you find your resting heart rate is extremely high one morning, you may need to readjust your training, get extra sleep, or even take a day off.

A further indication of overtraining is an inability to sleep. Other signs of overtraining include feeling weak, tired, achy, having a headache, and being hot and sweaty. If any of these symptoms persist for more than a day or two, altering your training may be helpful. Tom Dolan, the 1996 Olympic gold medalist in the 400 individual medley, experienced overtraining syndrome

TREATING EVERYDAY SORENESS

Expect some soreness from everyday training. A hot bath or whirlpool, a back rub, a nap, or stretching may alleviate some of the pain. Taking aspirin or ibuprofen as directed is beneficial to aching joints and muscles. Exocaine Plus, a lotion with aspirin in it, can also offer relief. Once you rub it on the sore spots, the lotion and aspirin are absorbed into the muscle. If the soreness turns to more extreme pain, heat treatments prior to training and ice afterwards applied to the affected area can be beneficial. Continue this treatment throughout the year as a preventive measure so the pain does not recur. You may find that a few days of rest or a week off are necessary. You can always try to run or bike if you cannot swim. If the pain persists, or becomes too extreme, see a specialist.

Other treatments available include electrostimulation and deep muscle massage. You can do the electrostimulation with a portable Solitens unit if prescribed by a doctor or by a physical therapist. The Solitens unit does a good job of reducing the pain in the sore spots or trigger points. Only a few chiropractors perform deep muscle massage, in which the muscle knots are painfully broken down by rubbing across the knot, which gradually tears apart and dissolves into the blood stream. Plenty of water and ibuprofen are needed after a treatment. One of the most successful chiropractors for working with swimmer's shoulder and for helping triathletes, cyclists, and swimmers is Dr. Ferrell in Santa Barbara. His success rate is phenomenal.

and had to take time out of the water in January, 1996, just three months before the Olympic swimming trials. He still qualified for the U.S. Olympic team in March in three events. In August, at the Olympics, he did not swim as well as he or his coach had expected, because his illness had had a long-term effect. Paying attention to your body is vital to success in athletics and to your general health.

Balancing Your Life and Training

Finally, you need to adjust your program to your lifestyle. Many swimmers and triathletes have full-time jobs and/or families that require time and energy. Dave Scott was considered the best Ironman ever, having won the race six times. In the late 1980s, he retired from the sport due to his job and family commitments. In 1994, he returned, but with a different training program. He had to adjust his schedule to meet all his obligations. He couldn't meet all his time demands and had to separate himself from his family. Quickly, he returned to his outstanding form and finished 2nd in the 1995 Ironman. Dave had attempted to train at a high level, be part of his family, and maintain a job. He wasn't able to do all three, so he decided to leave his family in order to train. Each athlete has to decide what is possible and ultimately what is more important, and then make a decision. Dave had a supportive family and work, so it was possible to leave to succeed in his athletic goal.

It is imperative to adjust your schedule to keep order in your life. Without balance, the work or family pressures will affect your training and performance, ultimately. Finding a balance in training, family, and work is important for sanity and success.

Keeping a Training Log

When developing your training program, use the preceding as guidelines. In addition, you can ask for help from a local swim coach or attend a swimming or triathlete clinic. It is also important that you keep a log of your training. This log can help monitor mileage and the specific training. You can do the log by hand or on the computer. You can develop your own format or use the one provided in table 6.16. Include the following information in the log: your workout, including the mileage swum, skills practiced, sleep, and diet. You can also include how you felt about the training or record these observations in a separate log (see chapter 7).

A few training computer programs are available for swimming and triathlons. Check the current sports magazines for some, and experiment with them until you find one you like. One of the benefits of keeping a record is to help you through the rough days. If you find you have trouble every week before swimming in open water, you may still be uncomfortable or afraid of the medium. Maybe swimming with someone else or talking with an expert will alleviate your fears.

© Dave Thomas

Importance of Rest

For open water swimming and triathlons, training six days a week is sufficient and, in fact, taking a day off is essential for physical as well as mental recovery, especially if the intense training may last for a year or more. A scheduled day off gives you something to look forward to each week when you are tired, sore, or just feeling sorry for yourself; these are normal feelings for every athlete on some days. Resting your body weekly from the beginning of your training may prevent your body or mind from falling apart later in the season. It is true that many triathletes don't do this; however, many have retired from the sport for a few years and then returned. Taking a day off may prevent the mental and physical burnout and thus further your triathlon career.

Take advantage of each training opportunity; the success of your performance in a race or record swim depends on consis-

TABLE 6.16

Weekly Training Record Sheet

Daily Practice

Monday   Weight _____

Sleep _____ Resting pulse _____

Stretching _____

Swim mileage _____

Weights _____

Other _____

Tuesday   Weight _____

Sleep _____ Resting pulse _____

Stretching _____

Swim mileage _____

Weights _____

Other _____

Wednesday Weight _____

Sleep _____ Resting pulse _____

Stretching _____

Swim mileage _____

Weights _____

Other _____

Thursday   Weight _____

Sleep _____ Resting pulse _____

Stretching _____

Swim mileage _____

Weights _____

Other _____

Friday   Weight _____

Sleep _____ Resting pulse _____

Stretching _____

Swim mileage _____

Weights _____

Other _____

Saturday   Weight _____

Sleep _____ Resting pulse _____

Stretching _____

Swim mileage _____

Weights _____

Other _____

Additional comments on training:

_____

_____

_____

_____

tency in training. Be positive in training; look for the challenge and the fun. Remember, you *chose* to swim; you don't *have* to swim. This outlook requires consistent intense training. In practice, focus on what you are doing, such as developing endurance or monitoring your stroke and stroke count, not on how well you are doing in terms of time. The thrill of training is the continuous quest to improve and reach your goals. Chapter 7 covers techniques and tips to help you prepare mentally for training and racing in the open water!

7

Training
Your Mind

My 40 years of experience, as both a swimmer and a coach, have proven to me that 70 to 80 percent of any open water swim is mental. In any open water swim or triathlon, your body and mind are challenged to their limits. To be successful, your mind has to support your body. A swim presents many challenges: water temperature; weather conditions; tides; currents; marine life (fear of it); other competitors; goals; pain and how much to accept; loneliness; isolation; loss of hearing, sight, and some feeling; limited communication; how far to push yourself; and numerous other challenges. These challenges are the reasons why so few have conquered the English Channel or why being a great pool swimmer doesn't guarantee you will be a great open water swimmer. The mind plays a bigger role in open water swimming than it does in any pool race. Similarly, the physical challenge is greater than in any pool race. Few have the desire or the drive to push themselves to the edge for 3 to 10 hours a day, day in and day out, in the water, running, and/or cycling. This is why open water swimming and triathlons are challenging and exciting, and why your success is so rewarding.

Most of the English Channel swimmers train in Dover, England, within the protected harbor before their swim. Practicing in calm water didn't make sense to me, so I decided to train in the open sea off the coast of Folkestone, seven miles west of Dover. Daily

137

© Mike Griggs

New Zealander Philip Rush sets a record for a triple crossing of the English Channel.

I swam in rough seas and battled floating debris, changing tides, and obstacles on the beach. Most days the water was so rough I had to be pulled out by my mother. The rocky beach sloped drastically, and when the waves crashed into the shore, the rocks rolled down the beach. After a challenging practice, I could not climb up the rocky, sloped beach. Many days I was in tears from the conditions, from swimming alone, and from my frustration at not being able to get out of the water. Yet six days a week, for three months, I stood by the edge, swore at the cold water, and pushed myself back into the water. I reminded myself of my goal daily, to swim the English Channel and break the world record. I was training my body physically and mentally.

Just as you begin training for a swim a year in advance, your mental preparation must also begin at this time. If you are not prepared mentally, the successful swim or triathlon will remain a dream. A combination of realizing your motivations, focusing on your goals, reflecting on your training, engaging in relaxation and affirmation techniques, and learning to deal with pressure, fear, and injury is a vital part of preparing your mind for open water swimming.

FOCUSING ON GOALS

As discussed in chapter 6, after you have decided upon a swim or triathlon, you need to establish short- and long-term goals that are quantifiable, positive, realistic, yet challenging and performance based. Remember to write your goals down to make them more real.

By writing these goals down on a 3 × 5 card and referring to them frequently, you will better prepare your mind to achieve these goals. Recall that the first and most important goal is to accomplish a particular swim or triathlon. The second is to determine a target swim time, if the conditions are favorable. Last, determine a super goal—a target swim time if all the uncontrollable elements are perfect. You may add or subtract from these target times as your training progresses. Any swimmer or triathlete, whether new to the sport or not, has to make the first goal be just finishing the event. The second goal is optional for beginners. If you have no idea how you will do, use the first event to establish a base. From this experience, you should be able to evaluate which parts of the event went well and what needs improvement. This can lead to reasonable but challenging goals for the future.

Claudia had competed in swimming, running, and bike races and finally decided to try an Olympic distance triathlon. Instead of setting her first goal to be just to complete the event, she set a time and place goal. On the morning of the event, she didn't feel well but decided to still swim fast in the first leg so she could achieve her goal. She overtaxed herself and finally had to quit the race. After re-evaluating her performance, she decided in her second triathlon just to finish the event and not worry about her time or place. She finished the event and had a respectable time and place. From this event, she was able to establish reasonable time goals with a 5 to 10 percent improvement, based on her decision to train a little faster and a few more days a week.

Remember to stay flexible and re-evaluate your goals every few weeks. If you use outcome goals such as a place in a race, you only have partial control over the outcome. Performance goals, such as to improve the first half of the swim, break your time by 10 minutes, or keep your stroke throughout the swim, for example, give you more control and allow for greater flexibility when adjusting your goals.

To illustrate this goal developing technique, in October of 1977, I left for Europe to begin my preparation for the English Channel. Before I left, I decided what I wanted to accomplish. My goals, written on a 3 × 5 card, were as follows:

1. Swim the English Channel (1 out of 6 make it).
2. Break the overall record (men's, 8:45; women's, 8:56).
3. Break eight hours.
4. Swim the Channel in seven hours.

I kept the card with me throughout my 10-month training and travel in Europe. To constantly remind me of these goals, I used red dots. Anytime I saw a red dot, I thought of my goals. To further encourage this, I placed red dots on my watch, alarm clock, suitcase, swim bag, and tape recorder, and in each room I stayed in throughout Europe. Beyond these reminders, stoplights, car taillights, and many other red signs or pictures inadvertently focused me on my goals. Using this method meant I thought about my goals three to six times a day.

MOTIVATION

Motivation is one of the most important ingredients to success. Consistently training and training well is imperative. Some days it is easy to get up early in the morning, and other days it is not. More often than not, the most difficult struggle is getting into the water. Even for world record holders like myself, this was always the toughest part. My thoughts drifted from how warm I was and how cold the water would be to knowing I was training longer and further than anyone else was so maybe a day off wouldn't hurt. In England, I never skipped or shortened a practice, but I wanted to on many cold days.

There are many different ways to develop or assist your motivation. Keeping an eye on your goals as illustrated above is the initial step. Strive to view each training session as an opportunity not only to improve but also to play and exercise; so when you are at practice, make the most of it. Do your best. Setting little goals for each practice, such as swimming one mile in 20 minutes during a 10-mile workout, is challenging and important. Relate each set to your goals. Frances, an older triathlete, had to know the purpose of every set I gave her. She wanted to know how it would help her achieve her goals. Daily we discussed this, but it helped her understand her training and helped her work harder in her training.

Try for best times on each swim, kick, and pull set within the required heart rate for the set. This doesn't necessarily mean race pace, but it can mean the race stroke count without the power in the stroke. Establish little rewards, such as a movie or a new book. Be innovative as you accomplish your practice goals. Each workout needs to have meaning. Remember, each set, drill, and practice adds up.

One Day at a Time

These aids assist in your overall preparation but may not help you in your daily struggle to get in the water when it is cold, when you are tired, when you want to do something else, or when you just don't care. To alleviate some of this mental struggle, just look at one day and then one week at a time. Promise yourself something special for after the training or agree to do only part of the workout. Nine times out of ten, if you get through the first mile or set, you will finish the whole practice. Within the week are six days of training and a day off. The day off is a special day; try to relax and do something fun. Make sure the day off is never too hectic; enjoy it! Try to take a half hour to an hour on the last day of training for the week to evaluate the week's work and prepare for the next week. This will allow your day off to be spent without thinking about training.

Positive Attitude

The statement "Getting into the water is the toughest part" is true not only for open water swimmers and triathletes, but for pool swimmers as well. In 1972, Mark Spitz won an unbelievable seven gold medals in the Olympics. The hardest part of swimming for him, according to his college coach, Doc Councilman, was getting into the water on a daily basis. Once he was in the water, he did fine; it was just forcing himself to get wet that was tough. It is often tough to get into the water because of the negative thoughts in your mind. When you are being negative, acknowledge the thoughts and then yell "stop!" Attempt to replace these thoughts with positive ones.

Remember that a bad practice or a mistake in a race is a learning opportunity; mistakes simply represent an opportunity for feedback. Every good athlete falters or chokes at times. Attitudes are nothing more than habits of thought. Repeat the positive attitude you wish to acquire.

Focus

It is also important to develop a focus when you train or race. Do you think just about driving or about having an accident when you drive? Start each practice concentrating on your stroke. This will help you forget about the water temperature and conditions or how much you are going to swim. If you have a goal for each mile, you can focus on this goal, instead of just swimming. When you are having a problem in training and can't concentrate, refocus. Go back to your stroke; try to feel the power in each arm pull. Do you focus on walking when you walk? When you are in danger, you focus from one moment to the next. The best focus is to think about what you are doing when you are doing it. Attempt this when you are having trouble getting into the water or pushing yourself in a practice.

Once you get going, your earlier struggle seems insignificant, even if it was just the day before or if it may be there the next day. Yet, isn't this part of the struggle against yourself? Why do this day after day for a year? You have to answer this. If you can't, you may not continue to push yourself. You have to enjoy not only the struggle against the elements, but also the even greater battle your mind and body go through, whether it is from pain, fatigue, exhaustion, or a slight loss of ambition. It is an awesome experience. From it, you will learn that you can achieve almost anything you want if you go after it. That inner sense of strength is worth every daily battle, injury, operation, jellyfish sting, and/or disappointing swim or triathlon.

Mike Pigg, a world-class triathlete for 11 years and the best in the U.S. in 1995, separates himself from his competitors before a triathlon and spends time focusing on his breathing rather than talking to others. By doing this, he reaches his "zone" and is able to perform on a higher level.

RELAXATION TECHNIQUES

Relaxation is the first component of mental training you must learn. Relaxation is important to ensure that your muscles are loose and relaxed for performance. You can't perform to your limits if your muscles are tight. Further, you need to relax your mind to be able to respond to your body, your competition, and the race itself. There are many types of relaxation; two are presented here. Find one you enjoy and which works for you. Besides the following types of relaxation, there are books and numerous tapes on Eastern philosophies, such as transcendental meditation (TM) and yoga, that may be useful. Use relaxation exercises daily. You can perform these before you get up in the morning, just before practice, after practice, or before you go to bed at night.

Basic Relaxation

Relaxation begins by sitting or lying in a comfortable position. Close your eyes and take three deep breaths, holding each breath for five seconds before exhaling. Gradually relax each area of your body, starting with your toes and working up your body to your head. Concentrate on first tightening and then relaxing each set of muscles. Once the muscles relax, your whole body can relax. Take a deep breath, tighten your feet, and hold this flexion for five seconds before exhaling and relaxing your feet. Next, tighten your lower legs and take a deep breath, hold this flexion for five seconds, and then release the lower legs and exhale. Next do your thighs, stomach muscles, chest, shoulders, arms, hands, neck, head, and finally your face. Take three more deep breaths, hold for five seconds, and exhale. Rest with your eyes closed for 30 seconds. This whole process should take five minutes.

Besides using a relaxation technique, you may want to listen to relaxation tapes. There are hundreds of different types on the market. I prefer ones with a person talking softly or just sounds of the ocean or a stream. You need to experiment to find which ones will help you relax. Most public libraries have these kinds of tapes, so you can check out several types and find one you like. This will save you from buying numerous tapes or CDs that you may not like and may never use again.

Visual Imagery

Another form of relaxation exercise uses visual imagery. Start by sitting or lying in a quiet area. Close your eyes and take three deep breaths, holding each for five seconds. Think of a place that is relaxing to you. This place may be a warm beach or a stream in the mountains. Think of the place and look around the area. What is the color of the sky? Are there clouds in the sky? What sounds can you hear? Can you hear water? Can you hear animals? Is there anyone else around? Where are you in this place? How warm or cold is it? How does this place make you feel? Take three more deep breaths, hold for five seconds, and exhale. Keep thinking of this place for a few minutes. Each time you practice this, you will get better.

Whenever you are nervous or tight, try using either of these forms of relaxation. Again, if these don't work for you, find one that does. Before a practice or a competition, find a quiet spot and do the relaxation exercise; this will help you feel better.

AFFIRMATIONS

Another technique for preparing your mind for open water swims is to use affirmations. This means putting problems, such as cold water, a bad shoulder, or the time involved in training, into positive statements, such as the examples listed below. Write the positive statements on 3 × 5 cards. Read each card five times before you get out of bed in the morning and five times before you go to bed. After each reading, listen to a relaxation tape for 10 to 20 minutes. This can be a tape with a person talking, sounds from nature such as the ocean or rivers, or whatever helps you be calm. Your subconscious does not know what is past, present, or future. You can convince this mind that the swim or triathlon is already over *and* you have accomplished your goals, just by working with affirmations and relaxation a few times a day for the whole training period and training consistently. If you aren't training well, your subconscious will know and interfere with your believing 100 percent in yourself. The mind has amazing capabilities for helping or hurting anything you attempt. For my English Channel swim, I used these cards:

1. For cold water: The colder the water, the more comfortable I become; the colder the water, the more relaxed I become and the faster I move through the water.

2. For my injured shoulder: Each time I move my arms, it relaxes those muscles; and the harder and faster I move them,

the more they relax, the more comfortable they become, and the faster I swim.

3. Swam the English Channel: I am 1,000 times more calm, excited, and relaxed because I have just *swum* the English Channel. From the moment I entered the water, to the moment I came out, I was in the water 15 minutes.

These cards played a significant role in my English Channel crossing. I swam the Channel in world-record time of 7 hours, 40 minutes, over an hour under the previous men's record. The water temperature ranged from 55 to 58 degrees, but the major obstacle was a problem with my left shoulder that required extensive surgery and eventually ended my marathon swimming career. With the aforementioned techniques, I developed the mental ability to overcome these difficult circumstances to swim the Channel.

MENTAL TRAINING LOG

Everyone needs to find out what works for himself or herself. One day a week evaluate your progress. Look at the upcoming week and plan your strategy for the week. Each night, write about your practice in your logs. There are two types of logbooks, the training log (see chapter 6) and the mental log. These can be kept as one log, but I prefer to keep them separate. Keeping them in one log may make it easier for you to look at what you are feeling and relate it to that specific workout; but I found that when I recorded training and mental analysis in one log, my thoughts after I wrote down the workout were different than if I just concentrated on what I felt and the struggles I had that day. It is true that many of the challenging workouts may have caused the struggles, but separating the logs made it easier for me to find new ways to conquer fears or anxiety.

In a mental logbook, it is important to write down daily what you thought about in practice. If you have a fear, writing it down may help you conquer it. Set a goal of dealing with this fear within a set amount of time—maybe two weeks or two months. List the athletes, coaches, therapists, and/or experts who can help you deal with it. Don't try to deal with everything yourself. Ask for help.

Other things you need to put in your mental logbook include your motivational level on a scale of one to five (with one being the lowest and five being the highest), the goals achieved in the practice, how hard you worked, and how well you concentrated in the practice. Also, write in both of your logbooks after a competition to help you evaluate the competition and decide on areas where you need improvement. After you write in your logbooks, take a few minutes to go over the next day's practice to help you get mentally prepared for it. If you have fears, deal with them then, not the next day when you might alter your training.

DEALING WITH PRESSURE

Other types of mental challenges you need to deal with include pressure, pain, fear, and injury. Pressure is something you put on yourself, or others try to put on you. You have to control the pressure instead of letting it control you. The great athletes don't let external pressure affect them, but have to work to control the pressure they put on themselves. Most great athletes are perfectionists; this can lead to great achievements but also to great disappointments. Learning how to deal with achievement and disappointment will lead to enjoyable and less stressful training and competitions. Focus on eliminating the pressure through relaxation instead of worrying about performing well or choking under pressure. A threat sets off a physiological reaction within the sympathetic nervous system of your body. This is automatic; the body thinks it is a life or death situation and shuts down to protect itself. In most cases, this causes the athlete's muscles to tighten up, which can lead to injury or failure. You need to relax and transform the adversity into a challenge.

Other types of pressure occur when you compare your performance with other people's performances or with your past performances. Remember that each race is different and has different conditions. Comparison to others is futile; on any single day, anyone is capable of a great or poor performance. Focus on what you are doing, not on others, a record, or money. Motivation has to come from within, because when you are cold, fatigued, or hurting, external pressures may not help you; they may not be enough to fight through mentally and physically.

When Lothar Leder competed in the Quelle Ironman in Roth, Germany, he was ahead of the world record. As the crowd kept telling him this, he yelled for them to shut up and leave him alone. He focused on how he felt and not on the record. He didn't want the pressure. He wasn't even wearing a watch; he didn't want to know any times. He became the first person to break eight hours in an Ironman distance triathlon, an amazing feat.

Lothar could have listened to the crowd or race officials and started concentrating on where he was, how much time was left to break the record, and what everyone's reaction would be if he did. He didn't. He concentrated on his run.

In rough conditions in a swim or triathlon or if you are having a bad mental day or are injured, you may give up so you can compete well the next week or the next competition. Plan for and be ready to accept this scenario. Focusing on a few major races can help. If you are too tired or injured, decide whether you will compete ahead of time, otherwise the problem will creep into the race and may force you to quit anyway. Each athlete has to listen to her own body and mind.

© Mike Griggs

The Australian Maroney family battle heavy seas during their successful relay crossing of the English Channel.

DEALING WITH PAIN

Pain can be classified into two types: pain from injury and discomfort or fatigue pain from pushing the body to its limit. You do not want injury pain, but you need to strive for fatigue pain, which means your body is working to its limit; it means you have reached the pain barrier and your muscles have fatigued. By understanding what the pain barrier is, you can overcome the fear of pushing yourself harder and break through this barrier. If you learn only one thing from this book, learn that you can break through the pain barrier without hurting yourself. When you are fatigued and feeling pain, you need to focus on your stroke and challenge yourself to work harder. Fatigue should be a cue to work harder. You need to acknowledge the fatigue pain and go beyond it.

There is a psychological fear of death or tightening up with this pain. This is a normal body protective device. Deal with it one stroke at a time. Most athletes have developed a habit of easing up when they sense this discomfort; this is a bad habit. You need to learn to relax, counter the negative thoughts, focus on your stroke when the pain hits, and smile, because this means you are doing well and have broken through the pain barrier. This breaking of the barrier feels as if you can accomplish anything you will ever try. There is still pain, but it does not bother you. You feel on top of the world. It also teaches you that you can accomplish almost anything in life if you fight.

In any practice, if you work hard and challenge yourself a little more when you think you have nothing left, you are practicing breaking through the pain barrier. On any set, you can race the last repeat, especially if you think you have already been doing that. Try to go one second faster than the last repeat or than your fastest repeat.

I once coached a swimmer who did not understand how to push herself. I stopped her in a 1,650 in a pool as she was swimming so comfortably. Together we worked to get her to push herself in a race. At the last dual meet of the year, she hit the pain barrier on the 10th lap of the 20-lap 500-yard freestyle. She fought through the pain barrier and didn't give in to the pain. She improved her time by 25 seconds, swimming a time within reach of the national qualifying standard; she had a chance of achieving this at the conference championships two weeks later. All of this was rushing through my mind as I hugged and congratulated her. She looked me in the eyes and said she had broken through the pain barrier but never wanted to do it again. She didn't ever do it again, but she had once.

DEALING WITH FEAR

Fear also can be classified into two major types—fear of failure and fear of success. Fear of failure involves spending time worrying about what teammates or other swimmers are doing instead of focusing on what you can do. An athlete paralyzed by this fear is so busy looking back over her shoulder that she can't look forward.

Triathlete Garrett McCarthy had a positive attitude toward other competitors. When he competed against a favorite such as Mike Pigg, instead of having a fear of failure, he would tell himself he was there to beat Mike Pigg. This made it easier for him. In eight years, he has won 33 triathlons. However, for most people, if they concentrate on others, they don't do as well. What happens

© Mike Griggs

Alison Streeter of Great Britain had swum the English Channel a record 36 times as of 1997.

when you are ahead of your competitor? Many athletes self-destruct. If your main competitor is having a bad day, many times the other competitors will also have a bad day. How many times have you watched a good team play a poor team, and instead of doing well, the good team's performance drops to the poorer team's level? This happens daily. You have to focus on yourself and not be concerned about your competitors unless it helps to push you.

Fear of success, on the other hand, involves not giving that little extra or taking a risk due to fear that it will hurt or people will expect more from you. Some athletes just back off, while others actually get sick or injured. Giving your all and succeeding is exciting. Giving your all and not succeeding can be just as rewarding, because you know you gave your all. The result is not the most important thing; it is the quest. Let loose, take a chance, and you have nothing to lose. Don't let the pressure of doing well interfere with enjoying the physical activity.

Karen Smyers, the 1995 world champion and winner of the Ironman, has faltered repeatedly at the Mrs. T's Triathlon in Chicago. She commented that she had never done well at this triathlon. This attitude may have prevented her from succeeding. Is it an attitude or is it an excuse? Does it affect her during the race? Is she consciously or subconsciously waiting for something to go wrong or overconcentrating on her body and thinking something isn't right with it? This overconcentration may cause her to make a mistake, get injured, or even quit the race, since she knows she just never does well in this race. If this is a pattern, she either needs to skip this race or attempt to figure out what bothers her, what fear prevents her from winning this race. Hopefully, once she does that, she can overcome her fear and win this triathlon.

DEALING WITH INJURY

Injuries can have a devastating effect on an athlete, both physically and mentally. Some common reactions include disbelief, anger, and depression. If you are experiencing disbelief or denial of an injury, you may feel as if the injury is less serious or will be healed in a day or so. When this does not happen, you may feel isolated and lonely. Anger is a natural response to the injury. Unfortunately, this may be turned inward to become depression or taken out on others. Depression is to be expected, because you may not be able to accomplish your goal for the season or your career; the volume, intensity, and duration of the training you did may now feel as if it was wasted effort and time; or you might worry how much it may take to return to the level of training and success you had achieved before the injury. These are just a few of many reasons for you to feel depressed.

Some athletes accept injuries, whereas others don't. Some are simply not psychologically ready to return to practice or competition after the physical healing has occurred. Fears, anxieties, and doubts can surface. You may fear further injury. This can lead to re-injury or an injury to another part of the body. In addition, the loss of fitness (whether real or imagined) can make getting back in the water and rebuilding very challenging. Some fitness is lost after three days out of the water, but the training effect can last on some levels for two to four weeks. This means some fitness is lost, but because of the former training, it is easier to get back in shape quicker.

To deal with these problems when you are injured, your mind has to be rehabilitated. Rehabilitation can occur if you are around positive people and discuss your fears and anxieties with experts. Remember to write them down in your log and deal with them. If, on the other hand, these feelings are allowed to remain internal, your fears will grow. Discussion usually relieves these fears. Also, you have to understand the injury and all aspects of the rehabilitation to recapture self-control and a sense of managing the healing process.

Further, look at an injury as a growth period in which you are developing mental toughness. One of the best ways to develop this toughness is to mentally rehearse training daily by visualizing yourself as already recovered from the injury. At the same time, correct any weak links in your stroke or training. If you practice visualization daily, you will return to training with a more positive attitude, perhaps a better stroke, and a stronger appreciation of the mental role in athletics. This will enhance your training and competition.

Mental training is a daily process. It involves setting goals, affirming the goals daily in practice, and mentally working on motivation through positive attitudes, thoughts, and action, and dealing with pressure, fear, and possibly injury. You must mentally prepare for every event as you physically prepare. You cannot reach your highest potential as an athlete without mental and physical training throughout each phase of your training plan. If you prepare for a race, you have to prepare for every occurrence which can happen during a race. With regard to competitors, this means race tactics that are discussed in chapter 8.

8

Race Tactics

R ace tactics can be the difference between a success-ful race or a disastrous one. You must have a race plan, be able to watch and react to your competition, and be prepared for any weather conditions. Many parts of a race have to be planned and practiced. These include the start, swimming in a crowd, drafting, pacing, and overall strategy of a race. Each is covered in detail within this chapter.

In the second 16-mile World Championships in Italy in 1995, Chad Hundeby had planned to take the lead from the beginning by sprinting the first five miles. He felt he could build a large enough lead to win the race. Unfortunately, the race officials were not enforcing the three-meter rule, and a pack of 10 to 15 swimmers were drafting off of Chad. The swimmers were all within a few feet of each other. Chad was angry but still kept leading the pack. By 12 miles, he ran out of steam and was passed by the pack. Chad had set his strategy, but as the race changed, he needed to adjust his strategy. He didn't, and it cost him his second world title.

In FINA races and U.S. National Championships, officials are supposed to be on the course, and in the 16 mile, an official is supposed to be in every boat. If the three-meter rule is violated, either by the boat or another swimmer, the offending swimmer is supposed to be warned. A second violation would then dis-qualify the swimmer. Unfortunately, violations are seldom called. The only recourse is a protest after the swim, but even a protest doesn't change the situation. In all other open water swims and in triathlons, officials aren't watching for kicking, pulling, or drafting. Since there are no rules against these tactics, swimmers will continue to use them. In the following pages, I describe these moves and how to counter them. Some suggestions may be offensive, but if you want to swim with the pack, you may need to draft, or protect yourself from an offensive kick or from a swimmer dragging off of you. When necessary, the information below is divided into information for open water swims versus triathlons.

MASTERING THE START

In most open water swims, the start—especially the mass start—can be very challenging. In many cases, the swimmers have to run down the beach into the water. There can be up to 100 swimmers in each wave. If there are more than 100 swimmers, there is usually more than one start. In races under three miles, this is normal. In some ocean events, such as La Jolla Rough Water and Waikiki Ocean Race, there have been up to

© Mike Griggs

1,100 swimmers. The race may be divided into waves, starting five minutes apart.

If you are not a good runner, be careful in this part of the race until you have trained and substantially improved. If you are a good runner, take advantage of this and sprint into the water. Sprint the first 300 yards to help put you in front of the pack. In some races, the competitors are lined up by their numbers. When this occurs and you aren't where you want to be, let the race begin, drop back quickly, and run over to the side or place where you want to be. If there is no current then you want to be in line with the turn buoy for a parallel-to-the-beach course or on a more direct course if it is an out-and-back race.

Practice running into the open water and sprinting a quarter mile to half mile a few times every few weeks. This should be done as an anaerobic set near the end of a practice, once your body is warmed up. To practice running and entering the water with a group of people, either get a group of triathletes or swimmers together, or practice on a crowded ocean beach or lake beach. If you swim by yourself or the beach is not crowded, you can practice running into the water after you come in for a feeding during your practice.

Beach-Parallel Swims

If the swim is parallel to the beach, after the run into the water, there is usually a 75- to 100-yard swim straight to the turning buoy. At the turning buoy, there is a 90-degree turn, and then the swim is parallel to shore. Until the turn, the swimmers crowd on top of each other. Before this type of swim, decide if you want to be in the middle of the pack or at the edges. If you don't mind kicking others or being kicked, be in the middle. If you like to have room to swim, stay near the back of the pack. If you are a fast swimmer, plan to start out quickly, so you can get to open water faster. As stated in chapter 4, some contestants will not be as nice as others and will kick swimmers behind them to keep them off their feet. If you are behind a nasty swimmer, just swim shorter strokes so you won't hit his feet.

Out-and-Back Swims

For out-and-back swims, the pack will take longer to separate. In this type of a swim, it usually takes about 500 yards before there is enough room to swim comfortably. For circuit courses or pool swims up to 2.4 miles, drafting will occur. If you are in the lead or leading a group, you will be dragging other swimmers. Give up the lead part of the time or swim a little bit easier so you have energy for a sprint at the end. If you don't, you will be working twice as hard.

Water Starts

In some mass swims there may be a water start (figure 8.1). If there is no assigned order for starting, plan to line up in front of the shortest route. Use the eggbeater kick while in line in the water to give you space to stay afloat and provide a strong push at the start. Keep your head up for a few strokes if you are back in the pack. There will be lots of kicking, starting, and abrupt stopping, so pay attention (figure 8.2). Again, if you aren't comfortable with the kicking and congestion, start on the edge away from the main pack or start in the back and be patient.

Figure 8.1 Swimmers at the beginning of 16-mile river race in Philadelphia.

Figure 8.2 Swimmers at the start of an ocean race, swimming to support crafts.

SWIMMING IN A CROWD

In a race with lots of swimmers at the same speed or with only one start for everyone, you may be swimming in a crowd for the whole race. Usually this occurs for races under five miles, so you should mentally prepare for this in every race under five miles. This way you can decide where you want to start and your strategy for the swim, so there won't be any surprises when you show up for the swim.

In this situation, you know you will be kicked, you will have trouble finding space in which to swim comfortably, and you may have difficulty navigating. Have a plan of action ready to deal with each of these problems. As stated before, you can alter your lineup position to be in the middle, the side, or the back. Second, when someone is kicking you or swimming up your back, ways to deal with this have been discussed in chapter 4. If you are deliberately kicked—a swimmer draws up his leg and then kicks you—you have a few options. You can ignore it and stay relaxed, try to swim away from this swimmer, or grab the top of his foot at the heel. If you decide on the latter, pull the foot backwards to your side as hard as you can. This will pull you by the swimmer. Tell the swimmer not to kick you again, or you will retaliate. Most times, this wards off anything else from a nasty swimmer. You can always try to speak with this athlete after the race. It would be better if you could just remain focused on your swim. In most swims you can, but sometimes you may be swimming among a few selfish swimmers; you may not be able to angle away or just stop. If you retaliate, return to your focus as soon as possible. Do whatever you feel comfortable doing which will not effect your swim focus or cause you greater problems.

Toni was a beginner triathlete with limited swimming experience. She enjoyed swimming but not in a crowded race situation, since she didn't like being hit or touched. To help her overcome this, I had one swimmer swim behind her, and one on each side of her in a pool practice, hitting and touching her constantly. Once she adapted to being touched and hit, we did the same in an open water practice. Once she overcame her fears of being hit and touched and imagining that this touching was a fish biting her, she felt better in her triathlons. She even set goals of going out faster at the beginning of the race and being in the main pack of swimmers.

When swimming in a pack, the person next to you may keep hitting you underwater. This may or may not be accidental. If you think it is on purpose, you can ignore it and stay relaxed, try to swim at an angle away from this swimmer, drop back from this swimmer, or as a last resort, retaliate. If you decide to retaliate, as you finish your entry and outsweep, instead of pulling your arm under your body push the hand back and under your opponent's chest. If you keep your elbow high, you will hit this person in the chest with your elbow. Normally this sends the message that you are not going to take this, and the swimmer will stop hitting you on purpose. Give the swimmer a dirty look to reinforce your point. Again, you don't have to do anything, but whatever you do, quickly return your focus to your swim.

If you are swimming in a crowd, just stay relaxed. After a few strokes, lift your head and look to see if there is clear water in front of you or on either the right or the left. You may have to wait a few more yards for the pack to separate or for you to reach open water. Gradually angle to the open water. If you start to panic, stop and lift your head. Take a few deep breaths while using an eggbeater kick to stay afloat.

If you want to get into clear water immediately, look at a right angle to the direction you are heading. Turn 90 degrees to the right or left, and swim out of the middle of the pack. Clear all of the other swimmers. If there are quite a few swimmers around you, swim with your head up so you don't run into anyone. Once you have gathered your composure, get back into the race. You can stay at the edge of the pack, depending on the limits of the course. On the other hand, if you want to stay in the middle of the pack but have become flustered, try doing a relaxation technique as you swim. Take deeper breaths and roll into your entry to help you relax.

If there is a turning buoy at the end of the course, take a few minutes to prepare for other swimmers crashing into you or vice versa as you round the buoy. Take a peek to find the best angle of attack. In many cases, you don't want to cut the buoy too closely, because you can be pushed into the buoy. This may be dangerous if it is an old or permanent buoy with things growing on it. You could be injured. If the turnaround is a pier, count on barnacles, and, again, don't cut the pier too closely. If the waves are strong, not only can you be pushed into a piling, but you could also be pushed under the pier where there may be old pilings underwater. Also, it will be darker under the pier, and it seems as if there are always more fish under a pier. There may also be fishing lines hanging from the pier or stuck to the pilings. The best way to handle all of these problems is to have a plan ahead of time and beware of turning buoys and piers.

DRAFTING AND DRAGGING

I discussed drafting in chapter 4 in relation to USS's and FINA's three-meter rule. This rule prevents a swimmer from being within three meters of another swimmer or a craft. The exception to the rule is for the start, turns, and finish of a race. As I recommended in chapter 4, draft in these places; it is to your advantage. Usually the start and finish are 1,200 to 1,600 yards in length. To lead during this time may not be the most strategic plan. If there are only a few swimmers or if the course is wide, this may not be a factor. If, however, the start and finish are narrow, then it is advantageous to draft, not to lead.

In races where there isn't a drafting rule, draft; it can save you about 3 seconds per 100 meters, which is a significant amount over 1.5 miles. Prior to the beginning of the race find a swimmer who is a little faster than you are. Line up behind or next to this swimmer. Keep track of this swimmer and follow him through the waves (figure 8.3). In order to keep the swimmer in front of you from getting angry, stop six inches to a foot behind his foot. If he slows and you might hit his foot on your entry, cut your entry short. If you have to, swim with your head up for a few strokes.

At the beginning you may have to sprint, but if you can draft later, you will have time to recover. The energy you conserve from drafting will afford you the extra energy to make a move

Figure 8.3 A group of swimmers drafting off the leader, violating the three-meter rule in the 1994 World Championships.

near the finish. You will probably be able to pass the swimmer you drafted off of throughout the race.

If in a race you are the swimmer dragging others, try to get away. A few hundred yards of all-out sprint may separate you from the other swimmers. If not, angle away from the swimmers or head slightly off course. Many times, this causes the trailing swimmer to take over the lead. When this happens, slide in behind the lead swimmer and draft. If this is a nasty swimmer, beware of his feet. If the following swimmer doesn't take over the lead, slow down. If the swimmer thinks you have "died"—too much lactic acid has accumulated in your muscles, decreasing your stroke power and stroke rate, causing you to slow down—the swimmer may pass you. If the following swimmer doesn't pass you, relax enough to recover and prepare for a sprint at the finish.

There is another problem with being the swimmer who is dragging others. It makes you frustrated and can make you angry. It makes you think of the other swimmer and takes your concentration off of your stroke and race. Practice having someone swim on your feet in training to help you learn different strategies to get away or to mentally deal with having to drag another swimmer throughout a race. If you can refocus on your stroke and try some relaxation techniques, you may not be as affected by the drafting swimmer.

When I was 14, I swam a three-mile junior national cable race in Nebraska. This was a quarter-mile course around a cable, 12 times. I took an early lead, and my competitor drafted on my feet throughout the race. Numerous times she accidentally hit my toes. I did not let it bother me, since I knew she had to pass me to win the race. At every turn I sped up, so she couldn't pass me. During the rest of the swim, I swam at 85 percent, making sure I had enough energy to sprint the last leg of the race. When I rounded the buoy for the last leg, I kept my sprint up and won the race. Two years earlier, I had swum my first cable swim and was the leader of a race, dragging a few other swimmers. This bothered me, and I used up too much energy and was finally passed at the finish. I had learned a big lesson from this and tried to never let this bother me again. When it did, I concentrated on my stroke.

In some swims there may be a lead guide boat. If this boat is less than 10 feet in front of you, try to stay in its wake (figure 8.4). Depending on the size of the boat, you may pick up a draft. The water may be a little choppier, but this might be faster. The lead boat may be motorized, so be careful of fumes. If you are too close or the wind is blowing toward you, the fumes may make you sick. If the water is choppy, try to swim on the downwind side of the boat, even if you are 15 feet behind it. This will also make it easier to swim.

In the first 16 years of triathlons, drafting was legal in the swim but illegal in the bike portion. In the new International Triathlon Union (ITU) series, drafting is legal in the bike phase. Many athletes were opposed to this ruling, since it changed the nature of the race. One of these was Michellie Jones, born in Australia and now living in the United States. In her years as a triathlete, she had 56 victories and two world titles. She felt so strongly about the new ruling allowing drafting that she not only vocally opposed the rule but also boycotted the 1995 ITU Worlds.

Figure 8.4 Swimmer drafting off of a boat.

She was under the impression that other top triathletes would do the same. But this didn't happen, and it cost her another world title. Since Ms. Jones wants to continue to compete, she has had to adjust to the direction the sport has gone. At the 2000 Olympics in Sydney, the largest audience and analysis of the sport will take place. If fans, athletes, and officials oppose the legal drafting in swimming and biking, these may be adjusted in the future.

PACING OVER THE LENGTH OF THE SWIM

Pacing is an important part of any practice and every race. Pacing means you conserve your energy at the beginning so you have enough energy to complete the practice or competition. If you are drafting off another swimmer, you will be able to pace a better race, since you will have more energy for the second half of the swim or whenever you decide to pick up your pace.

In order to prevent "dying"—going out too fast in a race—you need to pace each open water swim, regardless of if the swim is 1.5 or 21 miles. For the shorter swims—1.5, 2.4, 3, and 5 miles—the first sixth to quarter of the race needs to be controlled. During this first part of the race, swim at 90 percent of your heart rate maximum and your stroke count; you will know what these are since you trained by heart rate percentages and paid attention to your stroke count throughout your training plan. You should feel pain in your arms but feel as if you are not pushing too hard. Once you decide to speed up, increase your effort to 95 percent of your heart rate maximum. Your arms should be burning and you should begin to feel it in your chest. This is normal. In the final leg of the swim, increase your effort to your maximum. This means you must add your legs. Everything will be burning.

For triathletes, you can look at pace in a few ways. You can build up your heart rate in each leg: start at 90 percent and build to 100 percent in the swim, then start over in the bike and build up and do the same for the run. You can also build up by legs: 90 percent on the swim, 95 percent on the bike, and 100 percent on the run. New triathletes may have to drop these to 80 to 85, 90, and 100 percent. You are going to have to experiment in practice and races to decide which tactic you prefer. In one set in practice, you can swim fast from the beginning on the first repeat, and on the second repeat you can go out at 85 percent and build up to 100 percent. You can also practice going out fast and then ease up for part of the repeat, and then sprint at the end. You may also have to adjust your strategy based on your training or on how well you feel on race day.

In longer swims over five miles, you need to control the first sixth to third of the race. Swim the first part of the race at 85 percent of your maximum heart rate and your stroke count. Your arms will be burning, but overall you will feel as if you have a lot of energy left. In the second phase of the race, increase your effort to 90 percent. Push your arms more and prepare for greater pain. For the final leg of the race, increase your effort to 100 percent.

As you train at faster and faster speeds, increase the percentage of effort in each leg of the race. After a few years of training for a short swim, you should be able to begin at 95 percent and increase to 100 percent in the second leg. For longer swims, you should be able to start at 90 percent. As you improve your training, you might even begin at 95 percent. However, this will take intensity in practice and entail taking risks in a race.

Many triathletes aren't especially strong swimmers. Many triathletes, such as Greg Welch of Australia, are strong runners, whereas others, like Scott Tinley, excel in cycling. Both Greg and Scott have to pace their swim legs so they can do better in the latter legs of the triathlon. Swimming is a sport that relies more on the upper body, whereas running and cycling are both lower body sports. As such, swimming will not wear out the legs as much as running or biking but can fatigue them in longer swims, such as over two miles, since you need to use your legs for stabilization and some propulsion. For shorter triathlons, if you are a strong arm-dominated swimmer, it is possible to sprint the swim and not overextend the legs. This should not affect the rest of the triathlon. If, however, you are a leg-dominated swimmer, you will need to control your effort level of your legs, or the swim may deplete some of your leg power and affect the rest of the triathlon. Similarly, if your worst leg is the swimming leg, you may want to swim controlled at 80 percent throughout to conserve your energy for the other two legs.

RACE STRATEGIES

It is important to have a strategy for each race. You may be the same speed as another swimmer, but you may be able to beat this swimmer every time if you vary your strategy. A race is usually won by the swimmer who makes an unexpected move on the other swimmers. When this happens, first, you hope you are close enough to see the move, and second, you have to make a split-second decision about whether to go with the swimmer or not. If you don't go with the swimmer and he doesn't "die," the race is probably over. If you do go with him you must know you have enough energy not to "die" yourself. When a coach is on a swim, it is the coach's responsibility to decide if the swimmer goes with another or stays back before the surge to the finish.

Start Strategies

There are quite a few strategies for open water swimming. The first is to start at 85 to 90 percent and gradually increase your speed. Most swimmers follow this strategy. The second is to start out quickly, faster than anyone else expects. In most races, swimmers expect everyone to swim controlled at the beginning of a race. If you go out faster, all the other swimmers will be startled and have to change their race plans or decide to stick to their

original strategy. This can be a devastating strategy for you if you "die" later in the race or for your competitors if you get too far in front of them. If you surprise your competitors at the beginning, this can mean your competitors can't catch you without adjusting their strategy. If you are the swimmer being left behind at the start and happen to catch up with the other swimmer, keep up with the swimmer and try to pass before the finish. There is a chance, of course, that both of you could "die" if you expended too much energy to catch up with the leader.

The third start strategy is to go out slower than everyone expects. This may slow the pace for everyone. There is a chance someone else may decide the pace is too slow and take off in a sprint. This is a good strategy for you if you have a fast finishing kick. To defend against this move, you need to take control of your own swim if the leaders are going out too slowly. You need to take off quickly and set your own pace.

Pulling Away

The fourth strategy is to swim with the pack until the middle of the race. Once everyone seems to be feeding or in a comfortable pace, switch sides of the escort craft, while the boat drops back slightly to shield you. At this point, you can take off in a sprint and maintain this sprint for at least 1000 meters. If successful, this strategy can be devastating to the other swimmers. Many will give up and just swim fast enough to maintain their current position. To defend against this move by other swimmers, your crew needs to be constantly watching for it, and you need to be prepared to sprint at any time in a race. This keeps you close to a swimmer who decides to take off and gives you an opportunity to pass him or her later in the race.

The Finish

The finish requires planning as well. In most swims and all triathlons, the race doesn't end in the water; there is a run up the beach. As you are heading into the finish, you need to decide if you can run up the beach or not. In the ocean, you must also decide if you are going to ride the waves in or duck under the waves. If you are afraid of waves, you can watch the wave while breathing every stroke to one side. As the wave approaches, duck under it and kick toward the beach until the main part of the wave passes over you. As soon as this wave passes, pop up and start swimming in the back of the wave.

Once in shallow water, whether you rode the waves in or not, push off the bottom, kick, and streamline your body (dolphining) numerous times into the shore. At about three feet depth, stand up and run up the shore. Lift your legs high to clear the water. In the shorter swims, there may be many swimmers getting out of the water at one time. Protect your head from someone dolphining in front of you. Run with your arms at your side but with your elbows out a bit.

If the swim was over five miles and you are fatigued, use the last bit of the race to prepare for the run up the beach. If you are battling with another swimmer and know this person is a better runner, do a major sprint the last quarter mile of the swim to ensure a lead. This may also fatigue the competitor trying to keep up. Plan for the finish; many swimmers have been passed while running up the beach (figure 8.5).

Flexible Strategies

If a race is being held in less than ideal conditions, such as strong winds, choppy seas, rain, or a storm, you may have to

Figure 8.5 Finish of Seal Beach 10-mile.

alter your strategy at the last minute. If you planned to negative split your race but you have to fight for every stroke, you may not be able to follow your strategy. Rough conditions force you to be flexible. Again, you need to experiment with different strategies when there are rough conditions in practice to find out what you like to do the best. If you know conditions will be rough in a triathlon or an open water swim, you may decide to control the whole race and conserve your energy for the rest of the triathlon. For the open water swimmer, you may control the first half of the swim to see how bad conditions are so you don't overextend yourself. If it is rough, control your energy and just pick the pace at the end of the race. If conditions change for the better, you can pick up your pace.

In addition, you may not feel very well on race day. You might be tight at the beginning of the race; you could be getting sick or have eaten something that didn't agree with you. After warming up, you may have to adjust your race strategy to fit how you feel. Again, you have to be flexible.

If you are competing in a series of races in which many of the same athletes are competing, the other athletes will expect you to do the same thing in each race. Shake things up a little by changing your race plan for different races. This not only allows you to experiment with tactics, such as starting faster, starting at a more controlled pace, or surging midrace, but it can also confuse your competitors.

At the 1991 World Championships, in Perth, Australia, Shelley Taylor of Australia changed her normal race plan of swimming the second half faster than the first and began very quickly. In the first 2000 meters, she was able to build a 200-meter lead. Since she made her move before the swimmers reached their escort craft, the other swimmers' coaches couldn't warn their athletes. No one expected her to do this. Shelley maintained this lead and became the first women's world champion. She went on to win numerous professional races and world titles.

It is important to plan how you intend to swim a race and to practice your strategy numerous times in practice. Think about alternatives in case of a bad start, drafting, a different pace than you expected by others, feeling tight, or rough seas. Also, find out who else is planning to swim the race, so you know the type of competition and how each may swim the race, based upon the swimmer's past. Proper planning will help you have a successful swim. The next chapter discusses the swim itself.

9

Final Preparation

To be successful in your race, you need to thoroughly plan and prepare for the many elements that make up a competition. These include the taper before the event, your equipment for the race, your mental preparation for all possible conditions and occurrences, the race or swim strategies and tactics, the coach's responsibilities during the race, unsupported and supported race logistics, communication during the race, the prerace meal, and feeding during and after a swim. Some of these elements have been discussed in other chapters. In this chapter, we will thoroughly cover the swim itself.

TAPERING

As explained in chapter 6, the third phase of training is the taper period. The taper is important for rest; this allows for peak performance in the race, time for more intense mental preparation, greater sleep, and final preparation of equipment and people for the swim. The practices during this period are designed to maintain conditioning but not to exhaust you.

During the taper before a big race, double-check your suit, caps, earplugs, and each pair of goggles. Make sure all the other equipment is ready. Proper meals and sleep are also important during the taper period. You should eat extra carbohydrates and nap frequently.

SHAVING

Another important decision made during taper is whether or not to shave your body. For all distances, shaving is beneficial, because it helps the swimmer feel the water better (and feel faster in the water), and it has also been proven that the swimmer moves through the water with less resistance and therefore swims faster.

Most swimmers shave their legs, arms, and back for the biggest races. However, if you are a triathlete who will be wearing a full wet suit, shaving your legs isn't necessary, but shaving the uncovered areas of your body can be beneficial. If you are over 40 and/or get cold easily, it may be better not to shave, since the body hair may provide a little bit of warmth. In a short race—under six miles—shaving may assist you in another way; if another swimmer tries to pull your shaven leg, the swimmer's hand will slide off your leg.

Also, if you are a male swimmer doing a series of races, shaving for every race may not be desirable due to the problem of dealing with painful ingrown hairs from shaving. If you do choose to shave, always use soap or shaving cream, a good razor, and use short strokes on the arms and legs. Have someone else shave your elbows, the back of your arms, and your back.

PRERACE MEAL

During a swim and each part of a triathlon, you need the right foods to replace your body fluids and replenish your energy. You will need to experiment months in advance to determine which foods work for you in training (see chapter 6) as well as the week and the night before the race.

In the 1960s and 1970s, the protein-carbohydrate diet was used to first deplete your system of carbohydrates and then overload the system with carbohydrates. This involves four days of eating protein without any carbohydrates, followed by four days of mainly carbohydrates. Since the body is afraid the carbohydrates will disappear again, it stores more than usual as a precaution. This added store of energy helps a great deal during a marathon event; similarly, pool swimmers competing in three- to five-day nationals twice a year were using the diet. This diet, however, can play tricks with your system and should not be used very often. In the earlier stages of the diet, you may feel tired, and later your body may react to the carbohydrates being returned to the body. After the swim, you may have no energy for a couple of days. There have been some severe heart problems related to this diet. If you choose to try this diet, consult your doctor first.

For my English Channel swim in 1978, I used this diet. I had an amazing amount of energy for the Channel swim, some of which can be attributed to the diet. The next four days after the swim, I could not get into the cold water of the Channel. I was depleted. The problem was, the next Saturday I had been chosen to represent the U.S. in a 17-mile race at Lake Windermere. I had no energy in the swim, but still managed 2nd place. I was exhausted for three weeks.

In the 1980s and the 1990s, to avert the side effects of the protein-carbohydrate diet, most coaches discarded the eight-day diet and in its place adopted a four-day overloading of carbohydrates only. The carbohydrate-depletion portion was successfully dropped. This diet was just as effective as the original, without any adverse effects. It was so successful that companies developed products an athlete could use during the overload period.

You also need to experiment and decide what to eat on the day of the race before the swim. You can experiment with this before each long practice swim. Some suggestions include bagels, French toast, pancakes, spaghetti without a sauce, hamburgers, and lasagna. Carbohydrates are easily digested. Meals such as steak or chicken take too long to digest, so you may want to avoid these foods. During exercise, the body shunts blood from the stomach and from all the nonexercising areas of the body into the exercising muscles. If the stomach is full, this natural process is inhibited since blood is needed for digestion.

Once you find a meal you enjoy or a group of foods you like before a race, try it on several occasions before the long practice. It is better to have an adverse reaction in a practice than on the final swim. Eat your prerace meal three to four hours before the swim.

It is important to drink fluid in your prerace meal. This drink can be apple juice, orange juice, carbohydrate fluid replacement drink, or water. In addition, a glass of apple juice a half hour before a swim is recommended. Water will help hydrate you but will not provide energy. A carbohydrate fluid is ideal, if you have practiced drinking it in training before a swim or race.

PRESWIM PREPARATION

It is important for whatever your event that you gather your equipment at least two weeks before your swim to give you time to test the equipment and adjust the goggles to your face. For a long swim, you should have two of every piece of equipment you will use: suits, caps, and goggles. If you use earplugs or a wet suit, check these as well. An equipment list for swimmers and triathletes is presented in chapter 3.

After many months of training, the day of your swim has arrived. Believe in yourself and your training and relax.

Triathlete Preparation

For the triathlete, besides getting your equipment prepared and marked ahead of time, you have to deal with a few more questions: How far are the bikes from the water? Where is the changing station? Is the water too warm to wear a wet suit? What if the course is in a shallow lake in the summer with 85-degree water and an air temperature in the high 80s to 90s? This could easily cause you to dehydrate during a swim. You have to prepare yourself and your equipment for every condition.

Unescorted Race

In an unescorted race, whether a swim or triathlon, you need to take care of your own food, equipment, and planning. Ideally, a friend or coach should accompany you to the race and act as your support crew, providing not only mental support but also carrying your gear and clothes after the race begins. This person can have the towel and clothes ready for you at the finish line.

Make sure your support person has a ride to the race. The support person should pack the night before the race and lay out clothes to wear. Have the directions and a map detailing where you are going placed with your swim bag. It is also wise to be sure your car is filled with gas and that you have set two clocks (one plugged in and a wind up in case the electricity fails during the night).

Plan to wake up early enough to shower if you are tight and to eat a high carbohydrate breakfast. For the last time, check your equipment. Leave plenty of time ahead to account for an accident on the road or a flat tire. Needless to say, preparation is the key to staying calm on race day.

Arrive at least an hour and a half before the race begins. Check the course and then warm up. After warming up, change your suit, if possible, or put on a warm parka, and drink more fluids containing carbohydrates. If you are nervous or need to hear some positive comments, your support person can help calm and encourage you. Your coach or support person can go over the race plan with you to keep you relaxed and concentrated and provide any other assistance or emotional support you may need.

Figure 9.1 Mass start.

Paddler-Escorted Race

For an escorted swim with a paddler or kayaker, meet with your paddler at least once about two weeks before the swim. It is best if the paddler escorts you on a practice swim, so you can practice with each other. If this isn't possible, at least get together to go over the race plan, feeding, hand signals, and anything else you want or don't want in the race. In addition to driving or arranging a ride for the support person, you need to make sure that the paddler and craft will arrive.

You, your coach, a support person, and the paddler should meet at least an hour and a half before the race. You all should check out the course and then you should warm up. If you and the paddler have not worked together, this is a good time to practice. After warming up, change suits or put on a parka. The support person should give fluid and extra equipment—goggles, earplugs, and swimming cap—to the paddler. You, the coach, and the paddler should go over the race plan, feedings, hand signals, and positioning of the support craft at the start and during the race. The support person will take care of your bag and clothes while you drink fluids and relax before the race.

Escort Craft With Coach

For a race using an escort craft with a coach on board—most races over six miles—you will be able to rely on the coach quite a bit more for organization and controlling the boat. The coach will have your gear and food on board.

If you know which boat and captain you will have ahead of time, attempt to have a practice swim with the escort to allow you to get used to the boat and captain and vice versa. In most international races, the information about which boat you will have is provided a few days before the swim. During the practice swim, your coach has the responsibility to tell the captain what you and the coach want on race day. If a practice swim is not possible, your coach should meet with the boat captain the night before the swim, or, as a last resort, on race day as you are warming up.

Along with the preparation described above, you and your coach need to get together a few weeks before the swim to decide who will be responsible for what equipment and food, where to meet, and who's driving to the race. Again, the greater the preparation, the less stress on race day.

You, your coach, and your support person should arrive at least one and a half hours ahead of time. After you and your coach check out the start, warm up. After a 20- to 30-minute warm up, dry off, get warm, and drink some fluids. Go over the race plan, feedings, boat positioning, and communication signals with your coach.

About a half hour before the race is to begin, the boats will leave the shore and proceed to the pickup point. This point is usually 500 to 2000 meters from the start. You will need another person on shore to pick up your parka and towel, to hold an extra pair of goggles and cap in case your goggles or cap break before the start, and to hold your prerace fluids. The other spare equipment is in the boat with the coach.

Individual Swim

Normally, for an individual swim, a larger boat, over 20 feet, accompanies you, but this will depend on the length of the swim, number of escorts needed, and the size of the body of water. You will need to contact the navigator and arrange to hire the boat up to a year in advance. You will then need to meet with the navigator and pay a deposit for the swim.

The individual swim preparation can be divided into two areas: the support crew and the equipment needed. Both of these areas need to be organized weeks in advance so that everyone and everything is prepared. You and your coach must decide who will be responsible for the equipment, food, the support crew and their jobs, and communication with everyone. Often the swimmer gets all the equipment, arranges all the food, and finds a support crew. The coach gets his or her own equipment and communicates with the support crew and navigator.

Support Crew. The support crew—overseen by the coach—is vital to each crossing. With a good support crew, the coach can work almost completely with the swimmer—concentrate on the stroke, communicate at breaks, and be visible to the swimmer. The coach needs to develop a feeding schedule both for time and types of fluid and needs to have practiced these for a few months with you during the long swim. This preparation will assure a smooth and excellent swim.

When choosing a crew, select people who are physically fit and well conditioned. In some swims, a crew may be awake for 20 hours or more, so each member has to be in shape. The crew should sleep when possible and drink fluids throughout your swim.

The support crew can be divided into the land and water crews. The land crew is composed of three people: a coach's assistant, a food/equipment person, and the water support person. The coach's assistant aids the coach by making sure everything and everyone is ready when they need to be. The food/equipment person prepares the food and/or equipment for your breaks. Before the swim, this person puts the petroleum jelly or lanolin on you, and afterwards, assists you in dressing. A parent or good friend best fits this role. The water support person does a similar job as the food/equipment person, but does it for the paddlers and swim pacers.

The paddlers and swim pacers are the water crew. The paddleboards or kayaks guide you in the water and are used for safety and better communication. In some swims, paddlers or kayaks are illegal; in such cases, you need to guide off of the boat. If paddlers are used, two paddlers, one on each side of you, are ideal, but one is sufficient if you can guide off one paddler. Paddlers relieve you from having to raise your head to look for the boat. If a kayak is used, only one is needed.

By swimming next to you, a swim pacer can help you break the boredom of being alone or keep your speed going if you begin to falter. Usually the pacer swims for 20 to 30 minutes. If you need more support, a second pacer may take over after the first. Rarely is a pacer used for more than one or two rotations. Pacers are not allowed in most races and only in some individual swims. Some swimmers get annoyed with pacers, because the pacers have more energy and are faster than the swimmer later in the race. (I enjoyed the pacer. I always tried to sprint if I saw a pacer enter the water. My goal was to be fast enough that the pacer couldn't catch up with me. It made for a unique challenge during the swim.)

The support craft needs to stay at least three feet from you. In independent swims, there are no specific rules about drafting either from a craft or a pacer. A paddler should be close to you for safety. Depending on the paddler's ability, a two- or three-hour shift is feasible. When a kayak is used, this paddler can do a four-hour shift or longer, if necessary. For swims over six hours, I recommend a rotating shift of paddlers. Changing paddlers can occur just before or while the swimmer is breaking for food.

On swims during the day, a paddleboard or kayak and swim pacers aren't allowed, usually because there are too many boats in the area and the Coast Guard wants to limit the number of bodies in the water. (This is true for the English Channel.) A problem arises, however, when a swim starts in the day but continues into the evening. If there isn't a small escort, there is a chance the swimmer won't be able to see the boat. This makes feeding and communication difficult and can be very dangerous. Thus, a paddleboard or kayak is an ideal solution.

Equipment. Pack your equipment for the swim a few weeks before the swim. The equipment list is included in chapter 3. Check and recheck your equipment before getting on and off the boat.

It is also common courtesy to supply food for your support crew. Some food suggestions are listed in table 9.1. The coach's and crew's equipment list is shown in table 9.2.

One of the important items for the coach and crew will be some type of seasick medicine. If you or your support crew use this medicine, you or they should take it four hours before the swim (ideally, before the boat leaves the dock). The possible side effects are tiredness, confusion, and dizziness. Another option is a pair of Sea-Bands. These are wristbands that use accupressure to prevent seasickness. The Sea-Bands are a viable alternative to the medicine without the side effects of a drug. I have used them on numerous occasions with success.

The Coach's Role. For a swim under three miles, a coach may not need to escort the swimmer. In fact, in many races that are three miles or less, no support is allowed. If the race is over five miles, having a coach on the support craft is beneficial and, in some cases, essential.

If only a paddleboard or kayak is allowed and your coach is unable to paddle, you must find a person capable of paddling and train this person. Tell the paddler when you want to be fed,

TABLE 9.1

Food and Related Items for Support Crew

1. 2 ice chests
2. Premade (or the makings for) sandwiches—peanut butter, cheese, meat; bread, lettuce, tomatoes; mayonnaise, mustard, catsup, and pickles.
3. Lots of fruit
4. Lots of cookies
5. Lots of chips and snacks
6. Lots of drinks (mostly water and juices, some carbonated and caffeinated drinks)
7. Coffee, tea, sugar, powdered creamer
8. Hot chocolate
9. Napkins, plates, cups
10. Forks, knives, spoons

TABLE 9.2

Coach's or Crew's Equipment

1. Personal medicine (if any)
2. Briefcase and clipboard with action plans, feeding plan, information on swimmer
3. Seasick patch, pills
4. Pair of Sea-Bands
5. Rain gear
6. Suit, cap, ear plugs, goggles (2 or 3 pairs)
7. 2 towels
8. Bikini top (if female)
9. Shorts and T-shirt
10. Long pants
11. Long underwear
12. Sweats
13. Parka
14. Deck chair
15. Sleeping bag and large towel to put under it
16. Turtleneck and long-sleeve shirt
17. Tennis shoes
18. Socks
19. Emergency numbers
20. Camera and film
21. Moon boots
22. Squeeze bottle with juice
23. Hard candy
24. Fruit
25. Crackers
26. Swim bag
27. Press numbers
28. Communication board

what encouragement you want to hear, and where you want him to position the craft in relation to you.

Your coach is considered the final authority for you in the water. He or she is in charge of preparing and feeding you, monitoring stroke rate and stroke efficiency, and watching for hypothermia or other dangerous illnesses that can creep up during a race or individual swim. In addition, your coach must set the most appropriate course for you, watch for any dangers in the water, and keep an eye on other boats in the vicinity. The coach needs to continuously give positive support to you and keep a log of the swim. The coach is legally and morally responsible for your safety. There must be a bond between you and your coach; each needs to believe in the other 100 percent. This bond will occur with daily practice. Communication and support between you and the coach can make the difference between a successful swim and a failed attempt.

On an international trip, most countries require the coach to be cardiorespiratory-resuscitation (CPR) and first-aid trained, to have been on at least two swims of similar distance, and to have served on an open water committee. The goals of these requirements are to ensure the safety of the swimmer and to assure that the coach will be able to deal with any possible occurrence.

Preswim Informational Meeting. I recommend having each support person arrive at the boat about two hours ahead of departure time. Once everyone has arrived, the coach should have an informational meeting that you may or may not attend. You should know what is going on and add input if necessary. The coach needs to motivate the crew and help each focus for a successful swim. The elements for a standard coach's meeting are

- How the coach will direct the swim
- The order of paddlers
- How to guide and when
- When the swimmer's breaks will occur and what will happen during these breaks
- The rules of the swim
- The importance of sleeping and eating
- What the captain wants
- What you want on the crossing

Table 9.3 shows an example outline of this meeting.

TABLE 9.3

PRESWIM INFORMATIONAL MEETING

1. Coach's general comments

2. Paddlers

   a. List of paddlers
   b. How to guide
   c. Signals
   d. When to yell
   e. Shift

3. Swimmer's break

   a. Positive: no cold or pain questions
   b. Coach speaks first
   c. Lots of cheering
   d. Fluid
   e. Information

4. Observers and rules

5. Sleep and food

6. Swimmer's desires during swim

7. Captain's requests

   a. Where to rest
   b. Where to shower
   c. Where to go if seasick

8. Help of all for swim to succeed

The coach coordinates the swim. The coach will pick three assistants to help with the swimmer's food and equipment, the paddlers, and the food for everyone else. These assistants give the coach the opportunity to focus on the swimmer.

The coach explains the order of paddling throughout the swim and reminds each how to guide you and how little you will be able to see. The coach tells the paddlers who will be the head paddler and on which side of you the head paddler should be located. The coach reviews the stroke count signals and any other signals the paddler may need and reminds the paddlers to be positive and supportive but to limit their yelling, since you won't hear most of it and may get frustrated if you can't hear what they are yelling. The coach tells the paddlers how long their shifts will be and that they will be awakened 20 minutes prior to their shift. A normal shift is two to four hours. Usually, paddlers do two-hour shifts and kayak paddlers do four-hour shifts.

Prior to your planned break during a swim, the fluid or food is prepared and given to the paddler. Once the paddler has returned to his position, he signals you to stop and provides you with the food and fluid. The coach talks to you and relays information, such as distance or stroke count. Once the coach is finished speaking, others can comment as long as no negative questions or comments are given; in fact, at this time it can help if everyone cheers the swimmer. If all goes well, this break should only take 8 to 30 seconds. The swimmer finishes drinking, passes the bottle back to the paddler, or throws it to the boat. (I always found it fun to aim at my coach on the boat; it was a game that helped break the monotony of the swim.)

Next, at the meeting, the race observer explains the rules of the swim. This observer has the final say if anything goes wrong on the swim. He or she will disqualify you if you touch the support craft or do anything else illegal, and may stop the swim if the conditions are dangerous.

The coach explains the importance of each crew member's drinking fluids and eating during the swim and encourages each crew member to sleep, if possible, or at least rest as much as possible. Finally, the coach reminds the crew to use sunscreen during the day and to wear warm clothes if it is cold.

The captain needs to address where the crew members may sleep, which cabins are off limits, where to take a shower, and where to go if seasick. Normally, a seasick person needs to vomit over the side of the boat. There are two things this person needs to remember: don't throw up into the wind and don't throw up where the swimmer can see. If there is a danger of sharks, the captain will explain his plan to deal with the shark and how to protect you.

Another important item to be covered in the meeting relates to your needs as an individual swimmer. Being asked if you are cold or are in pain may bother you. You might not have thought about these negatives until asked. A crew member pointing toward something can aggravate you if you cannot tell if the person is pointing toward land, fish, or some problem. Eating or smoking by crew members may also bother you, since the smell hovers on the water. These items seem petty, but when you are in the middle of the swim, all by yourself, these little aggravations can hinder your performance. If they never happen, you have less to worry about.

Your coach should make sure everyone understands his or her responsibilities. Also, the coach should explain what he or she will be doing throughout the swim: watching you closely at all times, counting strokes, recording, communicating to you your stroke rate, making sure your food is ready on time, keeping in contact with the navigator, and checking that everything else is going well throughout the swim.

To close the meeting, it is a good idea for the coach to thank everyone for his or her time and energy, to apologize ahead of time if he or she yells, and spend a few moments encouraging everyone. The coach has to make sure everyone understands the major role each plays in the swim's success.

KEEPING COMMUNICATION LINES OPEN

Whether a single person or a large boat with a 10-person support crew is escorting you, communication is vital to success. Below, I present various options for strong communication between you and your support crew. Practice your modes of communication months ahead of the swim.

It is the coach's responsibility to keep in contact with you during both a practice and the race. Regardless of your age, a long-distance swim may affect your mental attitude. At the beginning, you may be happy and relaxed, later become angry, and then become quiet and distant. Your coach needs to keep the line of communication open during all of your moods. In addition, you and your coach should agree ahead of time that things may be said in the heat of competition that are not meant. It is also important to alert the boat captain and crew that this may happen and that no one should take it personally.

If the lines of communication are interrupted during a swim, you may become quiet and give up or drift into hypothermia. The coach needs to keep you communicating, whether through a look, a smile, or a word—anything to determine that you still understand the coach. Most swimmers prefer to maintain constant eye contact with their coach, and many get angry if the boat moves ahead or behind and they cannot see their coach. Your coach should maintain eye contact with you as much as possible, since the coach is watching your stroke technique and stroke count.

STROKE RATE

Your stroke rate or stroke count is the number of strokes you take per minute. This rate indicates your pace. Stroke counts should not vary more than three per minute over a 16-mile swim. A greater decrease in stroke count indicates that you may be in serious trouble. Since your coach has monitored your stroke count throughout the months or years of training, he or she should know your normal count and also how far your stroke count can drop before you have to quit. In the long training period, this decrease in stroke count probably occurred when you were sick, had an injury, or just did not feel like swimming. The coach should take the count every 10 to 15 minutes throughout the swim and communicate it to you directly or through the head paddler.

Grease or White Board

On a small boat, where you and the boat are only three meters apart, the best way to communicate is by writing on a grease or white board (figure 9.2). It is important to have a large supply of pens and a second board in case the first falls into the water. (Yes, this does happen occasionally.)

A grease or white board is one of the best communication tools the coach or crew can use to let you know your progress. Besides writing messages about positioning, time, and stroke count, the coach and crew can relay other information to you, including how far you have swum, what place you are in, how your stroke looks, jokes, encouragement, and anything else to keep you swimming and mentally alert. It is a good idea for the coach to have you nod your head or change your breathing pattern to signal when you have read the board. This way the coach knows you have read and understood the message. If not, the message needs to be rewritten or held up again. Your coach and crew should keep all messages simple, because long or involved messages may cause you to slow down or lift your head to read them. It may also be upsetting if you cannot understand what the coach is communicating to you. Practice this communication method during your long swim each month. After each long swim, your coach should ask you if you understood or could read all the messages.

Figure 9.2 Coach holding white sign board during practice swim, signifying a stroke count of 18 for 15 seconds and a mile swim time of 21 minutes and 30 seconds.

In a paddler-escorted or large boat-escorted swim in rough conditions, or if the board is lost, the coach or paddler may need a backup communication system. Yelling to you in the water isn't practical, since it is difficult for a swimmer to hear and this may force you to stop and ask what was said. A swimmer will get frustrated with this quickly and will quit listening. Using hand signals is one alternative.

Hand Signals

The preferred alternative to signs is to use hand signals (figure 9.3). Practice these signals months in advance of a race or individual swim. The following hand signals are the most commonly used:

1. Stop (left hand raised vertically with right hand on top of left fingers (i.e., time out)
2. Stroke count (closed fist then number, repeat twice)
3. Faster (thumbs up)

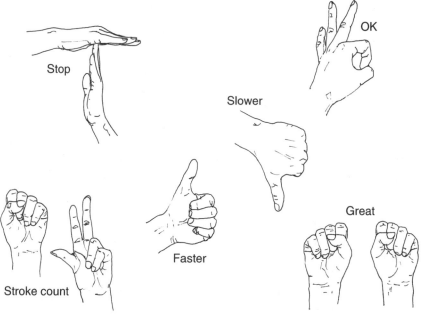

Figure 9.3 Hand signals.

4. Slower (thumbs down)
5. OK (thumb and first finger form a circle, three fingers pointed)
6. Great (two hands over head, closed fists)
7. Kick (move hands alternately, up and down quickly)
8. Stroke:
   a. Entry (elbow up, hand pitched down, in front of nose 1 1/2 foot)
   b. Downsweep (position as (a), then press hand down and out)
   c. Outsweep (hand at hip, press hand to thigh, and lift)
   d. Roll (rotate shoulders back and forth)
   e. Breathing (turn head and point to mouth)

To use a stroke count hand signal, you and your coach or paddler need to establish a stroke-count base for your stroke at some previous practices. This *stroke count base* is determined by taking your average stroke count during sprints and rounding that number up or down to the nearest 10. For example, if you normally hold a stroke count of 82 during sprints in practice, your base would be 80. If your stroke count during the swim is 84, you are in your normal base, and your coach will show a closed fist signifying the base is normal (i.e., 80) and then signify with raised fingers the rest of the number (i.e., four fingers in this example: 4 + 80 = 84). If your stroke count is 79 during the race, your coach will put a thumb down followed by a closed fist, to signify the base was not normal but less (i.e., 70), and then will hold up nine fingers. If your stroke count is 92, your coach will put a thumb up followed by a closed fist to tell you your count is higher than your base (i.e., 90), and then will hold up two fingers. Again, if your base is 82 and you swim 69 or 101 strokes per minute, the coach knows there is a problem and will stop you to ask what is going on. If the stroke count varies significantly, more than 10 above or below the base, this is a good indication something is seriously wrong.

If you didn't nod your head once this information is communicated to you during the swim, your coach should repeat the complete sequence until you shake your head. Often swimmers start out too quickly, and a high stroke count will alert the swimmer to analyze each phase of the stroke to be sure it is efficient.

If any of these signals are confusing or you don't like some of them, invent your own signals that are easy to understand and remember. You may add your own signals to the list, such as tapping your head if you smell fumes, alerting the coach to the problem and thus having the navigator move the boat to the other side of you. On a windy crossing, this problem may happen several times.

Talking During Planned Breaks

When you stop to feed or to speak with your coach, the coach needs to be positive and honest. If the coach has to ask a question, it should be an open-ended question rather than a suggestion, to allow you to convey what is going on in your mind. Rather than commenting on the cold or pain ("How's the bad shoulder?"), your coach may ask, "How do you feel?"

At least one month prior to the swim, the coach should know what type of information you want and how often. This may change on race day. For example, you might want to know where a certain competitor is; so everyone needs to be flexible.

When I swam the international race in Lake Windermere a week after the Channel crossing, I knew in the first mile I would not be able to maintain my normal stroke rate or push myself, because I was in too much pain. I was tied for first with my U.S. teammate. I told my crew, my mom and brother, just to tell me if anyone else was gaining on me, because I did not want to get worse than second. There was no way I would give up. I was fed every 20 minutes on the swim. We changed our race plans as soon as I knew how I felt.

GUARDING AGAINST HYPOTHERMIA

One of the most important communications your coach needs to have with you must occur at least two months prior to a race or swim. One sign of hypothermia is loss of reasoning and thinking ability, and one way to know if this is occurring is to ask you questions that require thinking. These questions need to be simple to answer but not something you would use in everyday conversation. For example, possible questions the coach might ask you are: Who was the first person you ever dated? What was the color and make of your first bike? your first car? What is your mother's birthday? What was your major in college? What was your favorite class in high school? Being asked your cat's name or your phone number at work is probably too simple to determine a hypothermia problem. Your coach should write 25 to 40 questions, get your answers at least two months before the race, and then not discuss the questions with you again. The coach can then ask them during the swim. If you can't answer one of these questions, your coach can ask another one. If you seem confused or cannot answer the second question, your coach has reason to stop you and get you out of the water as soon as possible to treat you for hypothermia. Your coach should make sure a medical crew checks you as soon as possible.

Frank Reynolds was 50 years old when he attempted to become the oldest person to swim the Catalina Channel. He trained well, but during the crossing had trouble drinking enough fluids. As he reached the upwelling water three miles off of the mainland, the water temperature dropped four degrees. The Coast Guard was called and an emergency boat appeared immediately. The skiff was put into the water as an extra precaution. Frank was able to answer questions, but his body position had changed slightly. The cold water gradually took its toll. Within a quarter mile of the finish, his stroke count dropped significantly. As his coach, I jumped in the water and swam up to Frank. I asked him who I was, and in a child's voice he responded my name. I asked him where he was and waited three seconds for a response as I studied his eyes and facial color. When he didn't respond, I immediately grabbed him and escorted him to the emergency vessel. He was rushed to a hospital and kept overnight. His body temperature had dropped to 89 degrees, and he had no memory of the last hour of the swim. He was released the next day and was back in the water within a day. Frank was less than 400 yards from the finish, but his life was more important than completing that crossing. The next summer, he became the oldest person to swim the channel, doing it in 10 hours and 34 minutes, a very respectable time.

FEEDING DURING SWIMS

Just as you need to experiment with prerace diets and meals, you also need to experiment to help you decide what to eat during a swim. In any swim over 30 minutes there should be feeding stops. This may not be feasible, but it should occur to ensure proper hydration. Liquid nourishment—such as a combination of electrolyte replacement and carbohydrates—is the most feasible choice, since it is easy to handle, easy to digest, and doesn't take much time to consume. If the water is cold or the currents are severe, spending time feeding can be detrimental. Drinking replacement and carbohydrate fluids is absolutely necessary for any swim over two hours or in the first leg of a triathlon over 30 minutes. You need energy to keep swimming. Some electrolyte and carbohydrate drinks include ERG, Gatorade, Metabolol, Endurance, PowerGel, Twinlab Fuel, and XLR8. (See figure 9.4.) How much and how often these should be consumed will be discussed later in this chapter.

You will need to experiment with the different types of drinks for three to four practices a week. Once you find one you like, use it for all future practices. The best practice to test the fluids is on the one long swim per month.

a   b

Figure 9.4 (*a*) Gookinaid and (*b*) Power Gel are a quick and easy way to get carbohydrate.

In the early years of open water swimming, swimmers and their coaches did not know as much about training and eating during longer swims as we know today. One of the most famous marathon swimmers in the 1950s, not only for winning races but also for his feeding habits, was Abo Heif. He ate a high-protein meal of three chickens before each swim, and during a swim, he drank fluids until he desired solid foods. On one swim, he ate two hamburgers and three eggs. Mathew Webb drank beef tea, brandy, and beer on his swim in 1875. As shown from these examples, our knowledge of nutrition has improved over the years.

In open water swims, the nourishment you need most as a swimmer is carbohydrate fluid replacement or carbohydrate load of 60 grams per hour, regardless of your speed. If, however, you are very small or large, you may need to adjust the amount. Most swimmers today consume a combination of carbohydrate load and carbohydrate replacement fluids. The current philosophy is three feedings of replacement fluid and one of carbohydrate load for any swim over two hours. You will need to experiment, not only for the taste of the fluid, but also for what your stomach will tolerate.

Normally, a triathlete drinks fluids or carbohydrate replacement drinks before a swim, but not during. For any swim up to 1.5 miles or completed under 30 minutes, you can get away without drinking during the swim. If, however, you never feel great near the end of a swim, you crash during the run of a triathlon, or the swim takes longer than 30 minutes, you probably need to drink every 15 to 30 minutes during the swim portion. Drinking every 15 minutes would be better, but having access to fluid currently is a problem. Obviously, carrying a bottle may be too much, but you may try carrying a PowerGel in the back of your suit. Take a quick break, and execute the eggbeater kick as you down the gel. You can also roll on your back and kick while you drink. Do this in several practices and see if it helps. You can also carry a collapsible water bottle.

For a 2.4-mile swim, you should drink replacement fluid and carbohydrate as discussed above a few times or every 15 minutes if the swim will take over an hour. Again, try the PowerGel or other fluid carried in a collapsible pouch similar to those used for cycling. You will have to carry more fluid, but this may make all the difference in your overall time or success. Similarly, in any unescorted open water races over an hour, use one of the above methods for carrying fluids and drink every 15 minutes.

Several hours into a swim, you may crave something other than liquid. Having a cookie, canned fruit, piece of banana, ThunderBar, or PowerBar may help relieve this desire and may also act as a reward. (See figure 9.5.) When choosing your food, take into consideration that in salt water, the tongue swells and it becomes very difficult to chew solid foods. PowerBar has developed PowerBites, small pieces of PowerBar; a few pieces may help to cut the salt when swimming in the ocean. There is a new product on the market, GlycoMax, which releases 80 calories of glycogen over three hours. It has received high praise from triathletes and open water swimmers alike. Again, experiment with the various liquids and foods during your long practice swims.

Figure 9.5 ThunderBar is a quick-eating food product.

In 1991, at the USS long-distance camp, the International Center for Aquatic Research (ICAR), under the direction of John Troup and with the assistance of his staff and graduate student, Marion Cassidy, of Florida State, had five athletes swim two four-hour tests in the flume (figure 9.6, *a* and *b*). They wanted to determine whether water or Gatorlode was the most beneficial fluid and what is the preferred timing of the feeding for a 16-mile swim.

In this experiment, each swimmer drank water in one test and 60 grams of Gatorlode in the other test. Muscle biopsies were performed prior to the swim and at the three- and four-hour mark to look at glycogen (glucose stored in muscles), muscle fiber type, and enzyme activity. Blood was drawn every hour and fingers pricked every half hour to look at glucose, free fatty acids, insulin, lactate, and blood gas. Energy cost analyses were done every hour to determine aerobic versus anaerobic contributions.

The open water swimmers' muscle fiber types were determined to be 65.8 percent slow-twitch and 34.2 percent fast-twitch. In the carbohydrate swim, glycogen stores were maintained in the first three hours. During the last hour, more glycogen stores were utilized. In the water swim, there was greater fat usage. Up to the third hour, there were few other differences. In the fourth hour of the water

a

b

Figure 9.6 (*a*) A swimmer being attached to a gas and air exchange system. (*b*) The swimmer swimming with gas and air system attached.

swim, there was a much greater increase in glycogen stores usage than in the carbohydrate swim. In addition, there was increased tissue trauma in the water swim.

In simple terms, these results mean that during the carbohydrate swim, the body used the fluid intake for energy, whereas in the water swim, the body metabolized its stored glycogen for energy. During the critical fourth hour in the carbohydrate swim, glycogen stores were being used but to a lesser degree than in the water swim. In the water swim, because of the depletion of carbohydrates for three hours, the body used a great deal more of its glycogen stores. The body became depleted of glycogen, and therefore energy. This verifies why some swimmers have crashed during the last hour of a 16-mile swim when using just water. Similar crashes have happened to numerous triathletes during the run portion of their event.

It is interesting that four of the athletes felt more dehydrated with the carbohydrate test swim than with the water swim, even though their bodies proved this wasn't the case. Only one swimmer drank carbohydrate first and water on the second swim. He fared well on both swims. The other four swimmers had water on the first and carbohydrate on the second. For three of the four swimmers, flume speed had to be reduced. They couldn't perform at the same level as three days earlier, and one had to stop completely. From this, you can deduce one of two things: first, these athletes can't do two swims within three days, or second, that the water-only swim drained too much from them, and their bodies weren't able to replenish their carbohydrate stores, and thus recover completely the second four-hour swim. The latter is exactly what the tests verified. This is just like driving a car without oil until it stops; if you add oil, the car may still work, but more than likely, the earlier driving without oil damaged the engine.

The glycogen level of one of the athletes was 150 prior to the first test and 50 at the end of four hours. Prior to the second test, his level was 100. Within the first hour of his second swim, the level dropped to 15. He was totally depleted; the test had to be stopped. In July of 1991, John Troup decided to test eight more athletes. These were given only one four-hour test, but the results were identical.

How Often to Feed

The next issue is how often to feed. You want to feed prior to your body's reaching dehydration or loss of energy. Feeding every 15 minutes is ideal, although conditions may prevent this.

Experimenting in the practice swims as you feel more tired will give you a good idea of how often you need to eat to maintain your energy level throughout the swim. The test at the flume didn't provide much information about the timing of feeding except that the 15-minute intervals between feedings of 6 to 10 ounces of water or carbohydrate replacement fluid or carbohydrate load seemed to work well. In both hot and cold water, shorter intervals between feedings seem to work best. If feeding is done correctly, the swimmer shouldn't lose weight during a swim.

Methods of Feeding

There are various methods for feeding during a swim. These include using a cup, hand, stick, bottle, or paddler. Once the feeding signal—a horn, whistle, or time-out sign—is given by the coach, you should stop to eat but keep the break as short as possible—between three and eight seconds. The navigator will move as close as possible to you and put the engines into neutral. As detailed above, the interval between feedings should be planned ahead, and the crew should prepare the fluid before stopping you. (The crew should prepare a second cup of fluid in case the first cup is dropped.) The crew should place the fluid in a cup or a wide plastic bottle. Cups are the easiest method when speed is important. Roll on your back as the fluid is handed to you. Chug the fluid, roll back over, dump the cup, and continue the swim (figure 9.7). This is the fastest way to feed and should take only four to six seconds. If the fluid is given by a stick, as soon as you stop, the pole should be extended to you; grab the cup without touching the pole since touching it is illegal, drink its contents, drop it, and roll over. A bottle can be thrown to you or handed to you in a net with a long handle. If a bottle is handed, the lid should already be removed. Regardless of which technique is used, a string can be attached to the bottle. Once you finish drinking, you can drop the bottle or put it back in the net and swim off.

If the paddlers are to change during a feeding, the old paddler returns to the boat first and the new paddler brings out the food. Once the new paddler is in place, the time-out signal is

Figure 9.7 Chad Hundeby reaching for two cups at the end of the 1991 Pan Pacific 16-mile race.

given. When a paddler or someone else hands the fluid to you, remember not to make hand or body contact. Drink, and then pass or throw the bottle back to the paddler or support person. In many races, you are requested not to throw the cup in the water. A string can be attached to the cup or to a bottle, so when you have finished drinking and drop the cup or bottle, the coach or support person can pull it into the boat via the string. You will need to practice feeding breaks to be able to do them quickly.

As you are drinking or eating, it helps if your coach tells you how far you have gone, what time it is, and how you look, and then encourages you. After the coach finishes speaking to you, a cheer from your support crew is a welcome encouragement. Many swimmers need more encouragement as the swim progresses and need to interact more often to stimulate their brains.

A quick note: If you have to urinate, the end of each break is the easiest time. If you have other problems, address them with your coach at this time.

REFUELING AFTER THE SWIM

Once the swim is complete, you will immediately need to drink fluids, take off your suit, take a warm shower, and dress warmly. If there isn't a shower, you need to be rubbed down with a towel. If possible, eat something and sleep prior to meeting press, family, or friends. This will help to replenish your system quickly. Following the swim, be sure you have carbohydrate replacement within the first 30 minutes. Juice, bagels, and/or fruit are excellent choices. Within 3 hours of the swim, you should consume a 100-percent carbohydrate meal and continue replenishing your carbohydrates for a full *24 hours* following the swim. Eating small meals or snacks may be easier for your system to digest than a large meal. Drink plenty of fluids to ensure a quicker recovery and to help remove the lactic acid from your system.

If you plan to celebrate after a swim, drink water and eat some food before you drink any alcohol. The alcohol will affect you quickly when you are fatigued. Further, if you have been in salt water, alcohol will burn your throat terribly, so be careful. A final reminder: It is also illegal on most swims for the navigator or crew to have any alcohol. It is very dangerous if people are drinking, and it puts the swimmer and crew not only in danger but liable for lawsuits if anyone is injured.

You are now ready for your race or individual swim. To be successful, you need not only to train and swim properly, but to taper, prepare mentally, practice feeding, have the proper equipment, and have a prepared coach, crew, and craft. You need to be prepared for anything and have a plan of action to deal with it. You need to have support to help you achieve your goals. With good support, you will be successful, regardless of conditions outside of your control.

The next chapter is designed to encourage you with accounts of some of the most famous open water races and triathlon swims. I hope it challenges you to attempt an open water swim.

10

Major Events

S anta Catalina, one of the eight Channel Islands, is located 22 miles off the southern California coast. In early February, 1919, William Wrigley, Jr. gained controlling interest in the Santa Catalina Island Company. Originally, he intended to erect "no trespassing" signs in order to have a private resort, but learning of the large number of tourists attracted to the island each year, he changed his plans.

The island, however, only had seasonal attendance. In 1926, looking for a scheme to build his declining profits, he issued an invitation to Gertrude Ederle, the first woman to swim the English Channel, to be the first person to swim the Catalina Channel. He was hoping to cash in on the worldwide publicity; however, she declined his offer. Wrigley decided to have a mass swim and offer $25,000 to the winner and $15,000 to the first woman finisher, for a purse total of $40,000. The swim, to be held in 1927, was to be known as the Wrigley Ocean Marathon. The race would go from Avalon to the breakwater at Point Vicente, a promontory landmark on the California coast. The straight-line distance of the Catalina, or San Pedro Channel, was 22 miles, 1 mile further than the distance to swim across the famous English Channel.

The race was open to all who entered, whether male or female. Even though no swimming test or proof of ability was required, there were many other requirements, including, for safety's sake, having a boat with a sanctioned official, safety equipment, and nourishment for the swimmers.[1] The race banned any type of artificial support. The wearing of a suit was optional.

The race, with 153 entrants, was planned to begin at 11:00 A.M. on January 15, 1927. All precautions against injury and illness were taken. The swimmers came from all walks of life, from all over the continent and the world. Thirteen women were entered. Many of the contestants were not true swimmers; however, over 60 of the greatest swimmers in the world were present. The entrants included Henry Sullivan and Charles Toth of English Channel fame; Charlotte Schoemmell, the first woman to swim around Manhattan Island; Norman Ross, holder of many national and world swimming records; Leo Purcell and Mark Wheeler of California; and George Young, a 17-year-old Canadian national champion. The other variety of "swimmers" included a long-distance runner and a teenage newsboy with no legs.[2]

Basically, three strokes were used: the slow but enduring breaststroke, the well-tested trudgeon, and the new speedy freestyle. For nourishment, each entrant had his or her own secret, ranging from chili to sponge cake. All felt anything that would add fat was beneficial. Replacing body fluids was the most important element, even if most swimmers didn't know this.

There were three ways to witness the race: at the start on Catalina, riding on Wrigley's steamer, or catching the finish at San Pedro.

Fifty-one of the original 153 entrants dropped out when the water temperature was announced—a chilly 54 degrees. Finally, at 11:21 A.M., the gun was fired and the race began. Slowly, the contestants entered the frigid water with the goal of becoming the first to conquer the channel and earn $25,000.

In the lead, unexpectedly, was George Young. About 20 yards behind was Norman Ross, desperately trying to catch up. Within the first hour, 30 more swimmers had dropped out of the race. Young, who was still followed closely by Ross, had changed his course, believing that if he fought a northeast current at the beginning it would enable him to ride a southern current into the coast. Unfortunately, this was not to be the case.[3]

By 3:00 P.M., 47 more swimmers had dropped out. Young, who was leading at that time, swam into an oil slick, which slowed him considerably. At 5:00 P.M., only 30 swimmers were left in the water. The contestants were spread out over 50 square miles, and darkness further hampered the officials.[4]

Young was in the lead by a half mile to one mile by 9:00 P.M. The conditions were ideal; a full moon was shining. At 9:45, only 12 swimmers remained in the water. By midnight, thousands of spectators began to gather at Point Vicente to watch the finish. George Young was five and a half miles from the finish; Ross was one and one half miles behind him; Clarabelle Barrett was in 4th, followed by Margaret Houser and Martha Stager.[5]

Within two and one half miles of his goal, Young saw lights on the shore. Thousands of people were flicking their car lights on and off and honking their horns to encourage the young man. At 3:05:30 A.M., Young emerged from the water, having spent 15 hours, 44 minutes, and 30 seconds on his watery journey. It was estimated that 15,000 spectators were on hand for the finish. "Bedlam broke loose afloat and ashore. Boat whistles, auto horns and human throats joined in a chorus, flares of Roman fire lit the scene and its background of rocks."[6]

Two women remained in the water when Young finished. Both quit after swimming over 19 hours. Houser had only a mile to go, while Stager had over one and one half miles to go. Neither was making any progress against the swift currents. Wrigley, upon seeing the dedication of these two, decided to give them each $2,500 for their valiant efforts.[7]

The Catalina race was significant as the first mass international open water race. There had been a few races in England, a 5-mile from 1877 yearly until 1939, a 15-mile River Thames race, and three races across the English Channel in 1904, 1905, and 1923. In each of these English Channel races, however, no one finished.

Due to the Catalina race's success in generating publicity, companies and numerous other organizations in quite a few countries decided on similar swims. This increased the popularity of the sport overnight.

CANADIAN NATIONAL EXHIBITIONS

The Canadian National Exhibitions began in August of 1927. In most cases, beer companies sponsored the swims. These companies did this for a number of reasons beyond publicity. At the start and finish, grandstands were erected for spectators. Fairs, parades, and parties accompanied the events. As laws changed, alcohol couldn't be sold on the weekend in Canada, except at a major public event. This exception was applied to the swims.

Immediately, professional races in Lake Ontario, Lake St. John, and Lake La Tuque emerged. Swimmers from all over the world entered these swims. There were races in Lake Ontario until

1964 and in Lake La Tuque into the 1980s, and there are still races across Lake St. John. Famous swimmers competing in these events included Norman Ross, George Young, and Lottie Schoemmel in the 1920s; Abo Heif, Greta Anderson, Florence Chadwick, Cliff Lumsden, Rejean Lacoursiere, Ted Erikson, and Dennis Matuch in the 1950s and 1960s; and Paul Asmuth, John Kinsella, Penny Lee Dean, Claudio Plitt, Chad Hundeby, and Shelley Taylor in the 1970s through the 1990s.

OTHER INTERNATIONAL SWIMS

In addition to races in Canada, three other major international races emerged: Lake Michigan, Atlantic City, and Capri-Naples. The Lake Michigan race was altered from 36.5 miles to 60 miles in 1963. It was one of the greatest and longest races in history. The race around Atlantic City began in 1954. The swim is 22.5 miles and is affected by tides, currents, and water temperatures. The Capri-Naples swim in Italy is an 18-mile swim from Capri to Naples, started in 1954.

Other exciting open water swims include the La Jolla, California one- and three-mile swims. Normally, over 1,500 swimmers compete in these races. In Australia, over 3,000 swimmers compete each year in a 1200-meter (.75-mile) race in the Lorne Pier to Pub Swim. Over 175 swimmers compete in the 6.2-mile swim in Indialantic, Florida. Finally, Seal Beach, California holds rough water swims with 1-, 3-, and 10-mile races.

NONRECOGNIZED SWIMS

While there is some interest for a long swim in a cage or a numerous-day swim, these events are not considered legal for a variety of reasons. While a cage may be necessary to protect the swimmer from sharks, this artificial aid is not legal by national or international rules. An open water swim is a challenge of a human being against the elements, the distance, and marine life. A cage lessens these odds. More importantly, the cage is attached to a boat traveling at or above 3 miles an hour, while few swimmers can race any significant distance at more than 2 to 2.5 miles an hour. If a swimmer is in a cage moving at 3 miles an hour, the swimmer is being pushed by the wave created by the cage. Even if the boat can be slowed with a sea anchor when the swimmer feeds and the engines have to be switched to neutral, there will still be forward momentum. Needless to say the swimmer will be pushed forward by this. Therefore, the swimmer is able to draft off of the cage and/or off of the boat and be pushed during a break. Likewise, when the swimmer tires and slows down, the boat continues to progress at the same speed. Drafting and propulsion are illegal in all sanctioned swims.

These swims may be interesting as stunts, but for the true open water swimmer they are not legal. If they were legal, then drafting, using fins, scuba gear, and wetsuits should also be legal, thus diminishing a true marathon swimmer's capabilities.

There are a few swims that take many days to complete. In these swims, the swimmer swims 4 to 6 hours, gets out of the water onto a boat, and rests. He returns to the water the next morning, repeating this process for a number of days until the contemplated distance is covered. While this may be an interesting feat, it isn't recognized as a legal swim. Obviously, the boat is again an artificial aid and the rest periods and change of activity benefit the swimmer artificially. As illegal swims, these types of swims are not pertinent to this book.

ENGLISH CHANNEL SWIMS

Beyond these races, the most famous races in the world have been the English Channel races. There were three early races— 1904, 1905, and 1923—in which none of the competitors finished the swim. Not until 1950 was another race held across the Channel. It was sponsored by the *Daily Mail*, the major British newspaper. Twenty-four swimmers competed in the swim, nine of whom successfully swam the Channel. The first race was very close; only 15 minutes separated the first two contestants. Since the two swimmers were separated by over a mile, no one knew who would land first or where each would land. Races were held throughout the 1950s. Greta Anderson swam in a few of them, winning in 1957 and 1958 and beating all the men.

© Mike Griggs

Alison Streeter on yet another crossing of the English Channel.

RESEARCHING A SWIM

After setting your goals and deciding upon your swim, be sure to research the proposed swim. For a triathlete, this information should be in your entry packet. For the open water swim that is a race, the information should also be provided in the entry. If the swim is a solo attempt, there are many avenues to pursue to research the swim. There may be a governing body that sanctions the swim, such as the Channel Swimming Association, which controls swims for the English Channel, or the Catalina Channel Swimming Federation for the San Pedro Channel. These associations have already completed the research, and all you need to do is contact them. (See below for information and contacts for various open water swims, triathlons, and related agencies from around the world.) If there is no governing body for your selected swim, then contact the local swimming agencies, the Coast Guard or Merchant Marine, fishing and boating associations, and/or local newspapers. A few books on open water swimming and triathlons have also been written and are included in the bibliography.

The more information you gather, the better your chances for success. Determine and investigate the distance of the swim, the average water temperature throughout the year, the currents, the marine life, and the availability of a capable paddler. For longer swims over five miles, gather this information almost a year in advance. If the swim will be in cold water (under 65 degrees F), a year of training may be necessary, regardless of the distance. Your background and swimming ability are the deciding factors.

Once you have gathered this information, seriously weigh it. Is the swim safe? Is the swim feasible? Is there sufficient time to train properly? Is there an expert to help you achieve this goal? Similarly, if you are an advanced triathlete or swimmer, go back to chapter 6 and determine if your seasonal plan is feasible and if there is sufficient time to recover between each major competition. If you answer these questions positively, then accept the challenge and commit yourself to completing it. If not, do not attempt it. Your life and those supporting you are more important than dying of hypothermia, shark attack, or lack of preparation. There is always another swim or triathlon.

SWIMMING AND TRIATHLON ORGANIZATIONS

The international body governing open water swimming is Federation Internationale Natation Amateur (FINA). FINA has an open water technical committee that establishes rules, sets up and sanctions international races, accredits officials, and keeps an eye on the development and potential inclusion of open water events in the Olympics. The first FINA World Championship was held in Perth, Australia, in 1991 and was 25 K in length. In 1996, the committee also approved a 5K race for world-championship status, so the 5K and 25K will be competed in all future world championships. In 1998, FINA began sponsoring a professional circuit.

United States Swimming (USS) is the governing and sanctioning body for all amateur swims in the United States. The open water committee controls the 5K, 10K, 15K, and 25K national championships. There is a national team coach and an open water coordinator for the sport. National teams and team members are chosen for each distance and for international competitions. Like FINA, the USS committee establishes rules and assists in development of the sport.

For further information on open water swimming races sanctioned by USS, contact:

Open Water Swimming

United States Swimming
One Olympic Plaza
Colorado Springs, Colorado 80909
719-578-4578
FAX 719-578-4669
Web site: http://www.usswim.org/

Open Water Coordinator
Dave Thomas
4506 9th Ave.
Rock Island, IL 61201
309-794-7519

Masters Swimming

Masters swimming also has open water competitions. U.S. Masters is the governing body for masters swimming. To qualify for masters swimming, you must be at least 19 years old. Each age bracket encompasses 5 years: 19 to 24, 25 to 29; 30 to 34, etc. The sanctioned swims include 1K, 3K, 5K, and 10K national championships. In addition, most older open water swimmers and triathletes train with a masters team, so doing this yourself can provide opportunities to find training partners in your area. To find a U.S. Masters team, contact:

U.S. Masters
Tracy Grelli
261 High Range Road
Londonderry, NH 03053-2616

Professional Swimming

Professional marathon swimming is guided by the International Marathon Swimming Association, IMSA. This association is made up of swimmers and race promoters from around the world. This group controls the administration and promotion of the Marathon Swimming World Series. In 1998, this group joined with FINA to sponsor one professional circuit.

The World Series is a group of races over 26 K. There are two seasons: June to September in North America and Europe, and January to February for races in South America, Australia, and any other Southern hemisphere races. For a race to be included in the World Series the professional rules must be followed and a minimum of $30,000 (U.S.) in prize money must be offered. A swimmer must compete in five races to qualify for the world title. Points are given for place finishes, and a world champion is determined at the end of the season for men and women. For more information contact:

S.A. "Sid" Cassidy
University of Miami
5821 San Amaro Drive
Coral Gables, FL 33146
305-284-3593

Triathlons

Triathlons are governed by a few international groups. These include the International Triathlon Grand Prix (ITGP), which has 10 races; the World Series Triathlon Corp. (WSTC), a new series of races; and International Triathlon Union (ITU), which has sponsored professional races. Triathlons are divided into the short, international, Olympic, long, Ironman, and ultraman races. Danskin also sponsors a women's series.

In the United States, USA Triathlon is the national body for triathlons. This organization sanctions triathlons, hires coaches, and selects teams to compete in the Olympic triathlon distances internationally. There is a national team and a training team in Colorado Springs at the U.S. Olympic Training Center. For further information, contact:

USA Triathlon
3595 E. Fountain Blvd. Ste. F-1
P.O. Box 15820
Colorado Springs, CO 80910
719-597-9090

1990 USA National Relay Team including English Channel world-record holders Penny Lee Dean (center) and Chad Hundeby (second from right).

SWIMS, RECORDS, AND CONTACTS

Open water swimming presents numerous challenges, whether the distance to be swum is 1 mile or 40 miles. The following is a list of some of the most famous and challenging open water swims and triathlons and the various contact people. Table 10.1 lists world record holders in various open water swims, with the years and times in which they accomplished their feats.

Open Water Swims

ENGLISH CHANNEL, ENGLAND

Distance: 20-mile swims
Season: July through October
Water temperature: 52–64 degrees F
Challenges: cold water, currents, tides, rough seas, ship traffic

Contact:
    Channel Swimming Association
    Duncan Taylor
    Bolden's Wood Education Unit
    Fiddling Lane
    Stowting Near Ashford, Kent TN25-6AP
    England
    011-44-1303-814788
    E-mail: 106463.2145@CompuServe.com

CATALINA CHANNEL, CALIFORNIA

Distance: 20.14 miles
Season: July through October
Water temperature: 62–74 degrees F
Challenges: currents, weather and conditions, marine life
Contacts:
    Catalina Channel Swimming Federation
    Frances Dean
    698 Birch Ave. N.
    Upland, CA 91786
    909-982-4317

LAKE WINDERMERE, ENGLAND

Distance: 13 miles
Season: June through September
Water temperature: 60–68 degrees F
Challenges: wind, cold spots, unpredictable weather
Contact:
    British Long Distance Swimming Association
    Maurice Ferguson
    16 Elmwood Road
    Barnton, Northwich
    Cheshire, England C8W 4NB

LAKE ONTARIO, CANADA

Distance: 32 miles
Season: July through October
Water temperature: 60–75 degrees F
Challenges: cold, winds

Contact:
  Bob Weir, President
  Solo Swims of Ontario
  78 Cameron Crescent
  Toronto, Canada M4G-2A3
  416-488-0527

MANHATTAN ISLAND, NEW YORK

Distance: 28 miles
Season: July through October
Water temperature: 60–75 degrees F
Challenges: rapid tides, currents, heavily polluted
Contact:
  Morty Berger
  c/o MIMSF
  56 West 71st Street #4A
  New York, NY 10023
  212-873-8311

FARALLON ISLANDS TO GOLDEN GATE BRIDGE, CALIFORNIA

Distance: 30.5 Miles
Season: August through October
Water temperature: 55–65 degrees F
Challenges: sharks, swift currents, cold water
Contacts:

Olympic Club	South End Rowing
524 Post Street	Hyde and Jefferson
San Francisco, CA 94102	San Francisco, CA 94109
415-775 4400	

COOK STRAIT, NEW ZEALAND

Distance: 13.5 miles
Season: February
Water temperature: 52–68 degrees F
Challenges: tides, strong winds, unpredictable currents
No contact.

LA JOLLA, CALIFORNIA

Distance: 1 or 3 miles
Season: September
Water temperature: 65–70 degrees F

Challenges: seaweed, over a thousand competitors
Contact:
LJRWS
P.O. Box 46
La Jolla, CA 92038

LORNE PIER TO PUB SWIM, AUSTRALIA

Distance: 1200 m
Season: January
Water temperature: 68–74 degrees F
Challenges: sharks, thousands of competitors
Contact:
Lorne Pier to Pub Swim
1 Backhaus Street
Hampton, Victoria 3188
Australia

SEAL BEACH, CALIFORNIA

Distance: 1, 3, or 10 miles
Season: July
Water temperature: 66–71 degrees F
Challenges: unpredictable ocean currents, rough seas
Contact:
Kirk Zuniga
P.O. Box 853
Seal Beach, CA 90740

Triathlon Swims

IRONMAN, KONA, HAWAII

The 2.4-mile leg of the Ironman is one of the most famous triathlon open water swims. This swim is an out-and-back course, 1.2 miles each way. The water is so clear throughout this swim that you can see the bottom and many interesting fish.

Distance: 2.4 miles
Season: October
Water temperature: 68–76 degrees F
Contact:
Rob Perry
813-942-4767

TABLE 10.1

World-Record Swims

English Channel (21 miles)
First: 1887 Captain Mathew Webb — 21:45
Fastest male: 1995 Chad Hundeby — 7:17
Fastest female: 1978 Penny Lee Dean — 7:40

Catalina Channel (20.5 miles)
First: 1927 George Young — 15:44
Fastest male: 1994 Pete Huisveld — 7:37
Fastest female: 1976 Penny Lee Dean — 7:15

Lake Windermere (16 miles)
Fastest male: 1990 Jay Wilkerson — 5:55
Fastest female: 1990 Martha Jahn — 6:03

Atlantic City (22.5 miles)
First: 1953 Ed Solitaire — 14:00
Fastest male: 1996 Stephan Lecat — 6:59
Fastest female: 1992 Shelley Taylor Smith — 7:00

Capri-Naples (18 miles)
First: 1954 Marei Hassan Hamad — 10:42
Fastest male: 1982 Paul Asmuth — 6:35
Fastest female: 1992 Marion Cassidy — 7:18

Lake St. John (18/24.8 miles)
First: 1955 Jacques Amyot (18 miles) — 11:32
Fastest male: 1993 Chad Hundeby (24.8 miles) — 9:19
Fastest female: 1990 Shelley Taylor Smith (24.8 miles) — 9:24

Rio Coronada (28 miles)
Fastest male: 1990 Diago Degano — 6:59
Fastest female: 1990 Sylvia Delotto — 7:35

Lake Memphremagog (21 miles)
First: 1956 William Conner — 19:14
Fastest male: 1995 Stephan Lecat — 8:13
Fastest female: 1994 Shelley Taylor Smith — 8:37

Lake Ontario (32 miles)
First: 1954 Marilyn Bell — 20:57
Fastest male: 1978 John Kinsella — 13:49
Fastest female: 1974 Cindy Nicholas — 15:10

Manhattan Island (28.5 miles)
First: 1915 Robert Dowling — 13:45
Fastest male: 1992 Kris Rutford — 5:53
Fastest female: 1995 Shelley Taylor Smith — 5:45

Cook Strait (13.25 miles)
Fastest male: 1962 Barry Davenport — 11:13
Fastest female: 1975 Lynne Cox — 12:00

TABLE 10.1 *(continued)*

Juan de Fuca (18 miles)
First: 1955 Bert Thomas — 11:17
Fastest male: 1955 Bert Thomas — 11:17
Fastest female: 1956 Marilyn Bell — 10:39

Bering Strait (2.7 miles)
First: 1975 Lynne Cox — 2:06

Farallon Island (25 miles)
First: 1967 Colonel Steward Evans — 13:46

Lake Michigan (60 miles)
First: 1961 Ted Erikson — 36:37
Fastest male: 1961 Ted Erikson — 36:37

CATALINA ISLAND, CALIFORNIA

This short triathlon includes a one-half mile ocean swim leg with some beautiful scenery. Besides huge orange Garibaldis (fish that look like goldfish), long seaweed should be visible near the island.

Distance: 1/2 mile
Season: November
Water temperature: mid 60s
Contact:
  Pacific Sports Corp.
  818-357-9699

ESCAPE FROM ALCATRAZ, SAN FRANCISCO, CALIFORNIA

You'll swim a cold, extremely challenging leg in the Escape from Alcatraz Triathlon. The 1.5K swim is in swiftly moving, cold (mid 60s) water. An exciting part of the swim is knowing that three prisoners tried to escape from Alcatraz the same way you are swimming. Also, you will be able to see the Golden Gate Bridge each time you breathe to your right side.

Distance: 1.5 K
Season: August
Water temperature: mid 60s
Contact:
  Scott Zagatino
  CS Sports Marketing
  310-453-5191

ANNAPURNA, NEPAL

In the Annapurna triathlon in Nepal, a 2K swim leg is held in Lake Phewatal; the swim is an out-and-back course. The turn-around isn't a buoy or a boat but a wall of a temple on the island in the middle of the lake. The triathlon is a high-altitude competition.

Distance: 2.0 K
Season: July
Water temperature: high 60s to mid 70s
Contact:
  Jan Turner
  Flat 4, 1 Hardwich Rd.
  Eastbourne, East Sussex
  England
  011-44-1323641388

MOUNTAINMAN, SEEFELD, AUSTRIA

The Mountainman triathlon swim is a 1.5K loop with a .1K run in the middle to turn around. The swim is held in a wonderful mountain lake with magnificent views.

Distance: 1.5 K
Season: July
Water temperature: high 60s to low 70s
Contact:
  Julius Skamen
  Rinnerstr. 7, A-6071
  Aldrans, Seefeld
  Austria

IRONMAN LANZAROTE, CANARY ISLANDS

Distance: 2.4 miles
Season: June
Water temperature: high 60s to low 70s
Contact:
  Kenneth Gasque
  Club La Santa
  Tinajo, Lanzarote
  Islas Canarias
  Spain

PORTO SEGURO TRI, RIO DE JANEIRO, BRAZIL

Distance: 1.2 miles

Season: June
Water temperature: high 60s
Contact:
  Djan Madruga
  Estrada dos Bandeirantes, 23, 480
  Rio de Janeiro, Brazil RJ-CEP 22785-090

MRS. T'S, CHICAGO, ILLINOIS

Distance: 1.5 miles
Season: July
Water temperature: mid 60s to low 70s
Contact:
  Jan Caille
  Capri Sports
  4001 N. Ravenswood Ste. 205
  Chicago, IL 60613

ULTRAMAN CANADA, PENTICTON, BC, CANADA

Distance: 6.2 miles
Season: August
Water temperature: mid 60s
Contact:
  Steve Brown
  604-493-6852

IRONMAN EUROPE, ROTH, GERMANY

Distance: 2.4 miles
Season: July
Water temperature: mid 60s to low 70s
Contact:
  Detlef Kuhnel
  011.49.9175-9600

2000 OLYMPICS, SYDNEY, AUSTRALIA

The newest triathlon with an awesome swim will be held in Sydney, Australia, at the debut of the triathlon in the 2000 Olympics. The women's race will be the first event of the Olympics. The swim is the three loop course (1.5 K) with an impressive view from the shore and the water of the famous Opera House.

Distance: 1.5 K
Season: September
Water temperature: high 60s to low 70s

CALENDAR OF EVENTS

For the general open water swim calendar in the United States and the major swims of the world, contact U.S. Swimming at the above address or Fitness Swimmer Magazine, Rodale Press, 733 Third Avenue, New York, NY 10017. For a general triathlon calendar in the United States and the world, contact U.S.A. Triathlon (above) or Triathlete Magazine, 121 Second Street, San Francisco, CA 94105.

GET OUT TO THE OPEN WATER

I have presented here just a few of the exciting swims and triathlons the world has to offer. When you find a challenging or interesting swim or triathlon, research it and resolve to accomplish it. Train both mentally and physically; work on your stroke; prepare your equipment, support craft, and crew; and eat properly prior to, during, and after the race. Develop a race plan with tactics and strategy for any possible natural or competitive situation. Decide on the best means of communication for the swim. Prepare in this way for as many races as you plan to accomplish, whether one or a series. Relax and enjoy each race. Do your best, and you can accomplish almost anything.

After failing in the Golden Gate swim, I planned for 13 years to swim the English Channel. The Golden Gate swim had taught me so much. I had learned to expect things to go wrong and to always have a backup plan. I had learned to prepare for a race almost double the distance and time originally planned, if conditions or other factors changed the situation. I had learned about tides and cold water. I had learned to understand the power of the mind and the mental side of open water swimming and to understand myself and my limitations. I had learned to research past swims and failed attempts. I had learned to appreciate the ocean and its inhabitants. I had learned to accept my failures and to learn from them, and I had learned to laugh and have a good time when I was out of the water.

From October of 1976 through mid July of 1978, I researched the English Channel. I met and trained with every major coach in Europe and spoke with anyone who had swum or coached anyone across the Channel. I began training in 50-degree water 10 months in advance to prepare for the swim. I trained in the Channel from May 1 until the swim in late July. I questioned my navigator, Reg Brickell, and the Scotts of the Channel Swimming Association, constantly. Each was helpful and supportive. Mainly, I trained up to eight hours a day in the water and another hour and a half mentally, six days a week. I swam in a pool and the ocean every day to maintain speed and endurance. I had a great support crew of family and friends, and on July 29, 1978, we conquered the Channel in record time.

Anything is *possible* if you prepare and believe in yourself!

NOTES

1. "Prepare Catalina Plans," *Los Angeles Times*, 14 December 1926, p. 1.
2. "Rabbit Punches," *Los Angeles Times*, 8 January 1927, Part I-a, p. 2. "Swimmers Set for Dash," *Los Angeles Times*, 13 January 1927, Part III, p. 3.
3. "Lad Wins Catalina Swim, Only One of 102 to Finish, Two Women Out Wear Goal," *New York Times*, 17 January 1927, p. 1.
4. "Canadian Youth in Lead Seven Miles from Goal," *Los Angeles Times*, 16 January 1927, p. 1.
5. Ibid.
6. "Lad Wins Catalina Swim, Only One of 102 to Finish, Two Women Out Wear Goal," *New York Times*, 17 January 1927, p. 1.
7. Ibid.

Appendix

Equipment and Assistance

BODY SUITS, SWIMSUITS, WET SUITS, CAPS, GOGGLES

Promotion Wetsuits, 416 Cascade Street, Hood River, OR 97031, 503-386-3278, 800-743-3796

Quintana Roo, 800-743-3796

Speedo, 6040 Bandini Blvd., Los Angeles, CA 90047, 800-547-8770

WaterWear Inc., One Riverview Mill, Wilton, NH 03086, 603-654-9885

OTHER APPAREL

Danskin, 111 W. 40th, 18th Floor, New York, NY 10018, 800-452-9526

Tru West, P.O. Box 1855, Huntington, CA 92647-1855, 800-322-3669

TRAINING AND RACING TOOLS

Coach's Scope, 800-762-6801

Power Reel, **Power Rack**, Total Performance Inc., 592 South Illinois Ave., P.O. Box 1268, Mansfield, OH 44901, 419-526-1010, Fax 419-526-0291

Sea-Band, Souwest Band Corporation, 400 Australian Ave. Suite 725, West Palm Beach, FL 33401, 407-832-5112

Simuswim 2000, Aquatic Advantage, 1434 Cola Drive, McLean, VA 22101, 800-666-6997

Solitens, Innovative Design, 3084 State Highway 27, Suite A10, Kendall Park, NJ 08824

FUELS

ERG Replacement Drink, Gookinaid, 8525 Suite L Arjons Drive, San Diego, CA 92126, 800-283-6505

PowerBar, 1442A Walnut Street, Berkeley, CA 94709, 415-843-1330, 800-587-6937

Bibliography

Allen, Mark. 1988. *Mark Allen's total triathlete.* Chicago: Contemporary Books.

Anderson, Bob. 1980. *Stretching.* Bolinas, CA: Shelter Publishing.

Burch, David. 1993. *Fundamentals of kayak navigation.* Saybrook, CT: Globe Pequot Press.

Campbell, Gail. 1977. *The world of the long distance athlete.* New York: Sterling.

Counsilman, James E. 1977. *Competitive swimming manual for coaches and swimmers.* Bloomington, IN: Counsilman Co.

———. 1977. *Complete book of swimming.* New York: Atheneum.

Dean, Penny. 1980. *History of the Catalina swims since 1927.* Pomona, CA: California State Polytechnic University.

———. 1990. *How to swim a marathon and shorter swims.* Colorado Springs: U.S. Swimming.

Edwards, Sally. 1985. *Triathlon—A triple fitness sport.* Chicago: Contemporary Books.

FINA. 1996. *Open water swimming guidelines.* Lausanne, Switzerland: FINA.

Maglisco, Ernie W. 1982. *Swimming faster.* Mountain View, CA: Mayfield.

———. 1993. *Swimming even faster.* Mountain View, CA: Mayfield.

Plant, Mike. 1987. *Triathlon—Going the distance.* Chicago: Contemporary Books.

Scott, Dave. 1986. *Dave Scott's triathlon training.* New York: Simon & Schuster.

Tinley, Scott. 1986. *Scott Tinley's winning triathlon.* Chicago: Contemporary Books.

Town, Glenn. 1985. *Science of triathlon training and competition.* Champaign, IL: Human Kinetics.

Town, Glenn, and T. Kearney. 1994. *Swim, bike, run.* Champaign, IL: Human Kinetics.

Wennerberg, Conrad. 1974. *Wind, waves, and sunburn.* New York: A. S. Barnes.

MAGAZINES

Fitness Swimmer, Rodale Press, 733 Third Avenue, New York, NY 10017

Swimming Technique, 228 Nevada Street, El Segundo, CA 90245, 800-352-7946

Swimming World, P.O. Box 863, El Segundo, CA 90245, 800-345-7946

Triathlete, 121 Second Street, San Francisco, CA 94105, 800-441-1666, www.TriathleteMag.com

Triathlon Today, P.O. Box 1587, Ann Arbor, MI 48106, 800-346-5902

Index

A

aerobic energy production 109-110
aerobic training 110, 114, 115, 119
affirmations 144-145
alcoholic beverages 18, 108, 196
alternate breathing 79-80
alternate-day training regime 119
anaerobic energy production 109-110
anaerobic training 111, 114, 115, 119
Anderson, Bob 101
Anderson, Greta 115, 200, 201
arm pull technique 72-76, 77-78
Asmuth, Paul 200, 210
Atlantic City swims 115, 200, 210

B

Babishoff, Bill 110
back-eddies 20
Barrett, Clarabelle 199
Bering Strait swims 1-2, 211
boats. *See* support craft; *specific types of boats*
body fat, and hypothermia 10, 12
body position, for freestyle 70-71
body roll, for freestyle 71-72
body suits 31, 216
breathing patterns 79-81, 82, 90
buoys and markers 47, 49, 50-51, 159
Burch, David 56-57
Burton, Karen 28, 40

C

cage, swims in 200-201
calendar of events, how to get 214
calisthenics 98, 99, 100-101
Canadian National Exhibitions 199-200
canoes 40-41, 173-174, 194-195
Capri-Naples swims 200, 210
caps 12, 34-35, 216
carbohydrates 107, 169-171, 188-190, 196, 216
Cassidy, Marion 191, 210
Catalina (San Pedro) Channel swims
  information for swimmers 207
  navigation 57-58, 61-65
  specific swims and swimmers vi, 1, 16-17, 28, 33-34, 37, 65, 78, 115, 187-188, 197-199, 210
  time of day for 27
  training for 91-92
Chadwick, Florence 37, 115, 200
chafing 30, 31, 35, 37
Channel Swimming Association 24
charts 61, 62
circuit courses 53-54, 155-156
coaches. *See also* support crew; trainers
  communication during swims 43-44, 182-188
  dehydration prevention for 17-18
  paddleboard support and 39
  responsibilities 8
    with hypothermia 14, 15
    with individual swims 177, 179-186, 195
    with races 9-10, 172, 173, 174, 182-186, 195
    with training 7, 8, 83
  selection of 7-8
coach's scope 83, 84, 216
communication, during swims 43-44, 182-188
communication, preswim. *See* meetings
compass 59
competition. *See also* races; *specific types of competitions and races*
  distances for 2
  rules for
    alcohol and drug use 108-109
    distance between swimmers 53, 153, 159
    drafting 53, 159, 162-163
    equipment 10, 12, 29, 31, 35, 200-201
    multiple-day swims 201
    support craft 47, 51, 53
    tactics and enforcement of 153-154
Cook Strait swims 1, 208, 210
Councilman, Doc 141
courses, learning about 47-49
Cox, Lynne 1-2, 210, 211
cross training 101, 118
crowded conditions 155, 157-159
currents 19-21, 66

D

Dean, Penny Lee
  English Channel swim 9, 13, 21-22,
    52-53, 69, 79, 137-138, 140,
    144-145, 171, 210, 214-215
  other swims and races 4-5, 33-34, 161,
    186-187, 200, 206, 210, 214
dehydration 17-18. *See also* fluid intake
distances
  comparison/conversion table 95
  frequency of training and 94, 96
  for specific competition types 2, 94
  for training 117, 123, 132
Dolan, Tom 133-134
drafting 49, 53, 54, 153-156, 159-163, 176
dragging 49, 154, 156, 161
drills, stroke 70-71, 72, 74, 75-76, 81
drugs 109

E

ear infections 19
earplugs 35
Ederle, Gertrude 5, 37, 115, 197
efficiency, of stroke 69, 83-85, 86-89
eggbeater kick 90
endurance, and technique 69-70
endurance training 110-111, 114, 119,
  123
English Channel swims
  by Dean 9, 13, 21-22, 52-53, 69, 79,
    137-138, 140, 144-145, 171,
    210, 214-215
  diet before 171
  history of 199, 201
  information for swimmers 206-207
  by other swimmers vi, 1, 3-4, 17, 24,
    37, 115, 138, 147, 149, 199,
    201, 202
  tides and 24
  time of day for 27
  training for 137-138, 140, 144-145
  world-record 68, 145, 210
equipment 29-45. *See also* support craft
  caps 12, 34-35, 216
  for communication 43-44, 183-184
  earplugs 35
  final preparation of 37-39, 172, 176-
    178
  goggles 33-34, 172, 216
  grease 12, 35-37
  for hypothermia prevention 10, 12
  lists of 38, 44-45, 177-178
  for navigation 44, 59-60, 61
  sources listed 216
  suits 10, 12, 29-33, 216
  for support crew 177-178
  for swim training 83, 84, 119, 122, 216
  for weight training 100, 101
Erikson, Ted 200, 211

F

family life 134
family members, as trainers 8-10
Farallon Islands swims 208, 211
Farley, Bruce 4-5
fat, body 10, 12
fat, dietary 107
fatigue, dealing with 148-149
fear, dealing with 149-150
Federation Internationale de Natation
  Amateur (FINA) 29, 35, 51, 94,
  153, 203, 205
feeding during swims 39, 40, 53, 181,
  188-195
finish strategies 166-167
fish 25, 26, 55
flexibility training 102-106, 118, 119
floating 85
fluid intake 14, 17-18, 96, 108, 171,
  181, 188-190, 196
flume, stroke analysis in 83, 85, 86-89
focus, mental 142
food. *See also* feeding during swims;
  nutrition
  for feeding during swims 188-193, 216
  for support crew 177, 178
freestyle technique 67-85
  breathing patterns 79-81, 82
  kick technique 76, 78-79
  stroke technique 70-78
    analysis of 83-85, 86-89
    correction of errors 81, 83-85, 86-89
    efficiency of 69, 83-85, 86-89
    endurance and 69-70
    for head-up freestyle 90
    speed and 67-69
    training in 124. *See also* drills
frequency of training 94, 96, 116-128
friends, as trainers 8-10

G

global positioning system (GPS) 56,
  59-65
goal development 91, 92-94, 139-140
goggles 33-34, 172, 216
Golden Gate Bridge swims 4-5, 208, 214
grease 12, 35-37
grease boards 183-184

H

hand signals 184-186
head-up freestyle 90
heart rate 112-114, 133, 163
Heif, Abo 189, 200
history, of open water swimming 197-
  202
hitting other swimmers 49, 50, 158
Houser, Margaret 199
Huisveld, Pete 56, 65, 78, 83, 85, 86-
  89, 210

Huisveld marking system 56, 64-65
Hundeby, Chad vi, 28, 43, 114, 153, 195, 200, 206, 210
hydration. *See* dehydration; fluid intake
hypothermia 1, 9, 14-17, 21
 evaluating during swims 15, 187-188
 prevention techniques 10, 12, 31, 35-36
 rewarming techniques 14, 15, 16, 196
 symptoms of 14-16, 187

I
imagery 143-144
Indialantic swim 200
individual swims
 coach's role with 177-179
 communication during 43-44, 182-188
 equipment for 176-177. *See also* equipment
 feeding during 39, 40, 53, 181, 188-195
 final preparation for 175-182
 postswim procedures 14, 15, 196
 preswim meeting for 179-182
 sources of information on 202-203, 206-209
 support craft for 43, 175. *See also* support craft
 support crew for 175-176, 180-181. *See also* support crew
 world records 210-211
injuries 78, 133, 144-145, 148, 150-151
intensity of training 109-114
International Center for Aquatic Research (ICAR) 83, 85, 86-89, 191-193
International Marathon Swimming Association (IMSA) 204-205
International Triathlon Grand Prix (ITGP) 205
International Triathlon Union (ITU) 162, 205
Ironman triathlons v, 2, 209, 212, 213
 specific athletes in 18, 134, 146-147, 150

J
Jaeger, Tom 110
Jahn, Martha 28, 210
jellyfish 23, 25
job commitments 134
Jones, Michellie 162-163

K
kayaks 41-42, 55-56, 59, 173-174, 176, 177
kicking other swimmers 49-50, 154, 155, 156, 157-158
kick technique 76, 78-79, 90
Kinsella, John 115, 200, 210

L
La Jolla swims 154-155, 200, 208-209
Lake Michigan swims 200, 211
Lake Ontario swims 199-200, 207-208, 210
Lake St. John swims 115, 199, 200, 210
lake swimming safety 20-21, 25, 26, 27
Lake Windermere race 186-187, 207, 210
landmarks 19, 27
Leder, Lothar 146-147
leeches 26
light systems 54-55
Lindbloom, Amy 114
line-of-sight navigation 57-58
logs, training 134-135, 136, 145-146
long distance swimming 2, 31
loran system 59
Lorne Pier to Pub Swim 200, 209

M
machines, training 100, 101, 119, 122, 216
Maglisco, Ernie 76, 110
Manhattan Island swims 198, 208, 210
marathon swimming 2, 36, 204-205
marine life 23, 25-26, 55, 181
markers 47, 49, 50-51, 57
Maroney family 147
masters competitions 35, 204
McCarthy, Garrett 149
McConica, Jim 28
meals, prerace 169, 170-171, 172
meetings, preswim 174, 179-182
mental training 137-152
 goal development 91, 92-94, 139-140
 relaxation techniques 143-144, 159
minerals 108
motivation 140-144
Mrs. T's Triathlon 150, 213
muscle fiber types 110
muscle soreness 133

N
navigation 46-66
 equipment 44, 59-60, 61
 getting to know the course 47-49
 techniques 49-65
 weather, tides, and currents and 66
Newby-Fraser, Paula 18
night swimming 27-28, 45, 54-55
nonrecognized swims 200-201
nutrition 107-109, 169, 170-171, 172. *See also* feeding during swims; food

O
ocean swimming safety 20-25, 27, 80-81
Olympic Games and triathlons v, 79, 163, 213

open water swimming
  defined 2
  history of 197-202
  reasons for participating in 2-4, 6
out-and-back courses 48, 155
outsweep 76, 81
overtraining 132-134

P

pacers and pacing 163-164, 176
paddleboards 39-40, 55-56, 59, 173-
  174, 176, 177, 194-195
pain 133, 148-149
parallel-to-shore courses 48, 155
Perkins, Kieran 114
Petranech, Dale 16
Pigg, Mike 142, 149
pool swimming 96, 114-115
positive attitude 141-142
powerboats 42-43, 53-55
power training 111, 119
practice swims 7, 8, 38, 39, 48-49, 81,
  174. *See also* drills; swim
  training
pressure, dealing with 146-147
protein, dietary 107, 170-171
pulling away strategy 166

R

races. *See also* competition; tactics and
  strategy; triathlons; *specific
  races and types of races*
  communication during 43-44, 182-
    188
  feeding during 39, 40, 53, 181, 188-
    195
  final preparation for
    equipment 37-39, 172
    nutrition 169, 170-171, 172
    prerace meeting 174
    shaving 37, 170
    for specific types of races 172-175
    tapering 124-125, 169-170
  getting to know the course 47-49
  history of 197-202
  postrace procedures 14, 15, 196
  sources of information 202-209, 214
  specific events 199-214. *See also
    names of events*
radios 43-44
reeds 26
Reetz, Erika 28
relaxation techniques 143-144, 159
rest 124-125, 133-134, 135, 169
Reynolds, Frank 187-188
riptides 22-23
river swimming 19-20, 25, 26, 27
River Thames race 199
Ross, Norman 198, 199, 200

rowboats 42
rules. *See* competition, rules for
Rush, Philip 138

S

safety concerns 7-28, 55, 181. *See
  also* hypothermia
  with support craft 41, 42, 51-53, 54,
    56
Salton Sea swims 115
San Mateo Marlins 4-5
San Pedro Channel swims. *See* Catalina
  (San Pedro) Channel swims
Schafer, Ute 111
Scott, Dave 134
sea anchors 42-43
Seal Beach races 40, 200, 209
seasickness 17, 177, 181, 216
seaweed 23
sharks 25, 181
shaving 37, 170
Shaw, Tim 110
shoreline, observation of 19
short distance swimming 2, 36, 57
shoulder injuries 78
16-mile swims 42-43, 68, 70, 124, 153
Smith, Shelley Taylor 168, 200, 210
Smith, Tobie 114
Smyers, Karen 150
soreness 133
speed 67-69, 114-115, 119, 122, 123
Spitz, Mark 141-142
Stager, Martha 199
starts 154-157, 165-166
storms 27
Strait of Magellan swims 1
strategies, for races 164-168. *See also*
  tactics and strategy
Streeter, Alison 3-4, 149, 202
stretches, for warm ups 12. *See also*
  flexibility training
stroke analysis 83, 85, 86-89
stroke rate (turnover) 67-69, 183
stroke technique. *See* freestyle technique
structures in water 19
sun protection 18-19
support craft 39-45, 51-56
  disabled 56
  drafting off 54, 162
  final preparation for races 173-175
  for individual swims 43, 175
  navigation and 44, 51-56
  on-boat equipment 43-45
  position for picking up swimmer 51,
    52
  for practice swims 49
  rules for competition 47, 51, 53
  for triathlons 9-10
  types described 39-43

support crew. *See also* coaches
  dehydration prevention for 17-18
  equipment and supplies for 177-178
  family and friends as trainers 8-10
  final preparations before race 172
  for individual swims 175-176, 180-181
  responsibilities
    feeding swimmer 39, 40, 53, 181,
      194-195
    with hypothermia 14, 15
    at races 172, 173, 174-175
    with sharks 25, 181
  sun protection for 19
  training for 40
swimsuits 29-30, 216
swim training 83, 84, 96, 116, 118,
      119, 122, 123. *See also* practice
      swims; training

T
tactics and strategy 153-168
  for drafting and dragging 54, 159-163
  flexibility in 153, 167-168
Taft, Ray and Zada 4
taper phase 124-125, 169-170
Taylor, Shelley 168, 200, 210
technique, swimming. *See* freestyle
      technique; kick technique
tides 21-23, 24, 66
Tinley, Scott 164
trainers 8-10. *See also* coaches;
      support crew
training. *See also* mental training;
      specific types of training
  coach's responsibilities 7, 8, 83
  evaluation of 132-135
  fluid intake for 96
  frequency of 94, 96, 116-128
  intensity of 109, 110-111, 112-114
  nutrition and 107-109
  partners for 111
  planning and scheduling of 115-135
  purpose of 94
  rest and 124-125, 133-134, 135
  supplemental training guidelines 97-
      106
  support crew and 40
  technique 124. *See also* drills;
      freestyle technique
  terminology for 125
triathlons. *See also specific triathlons*
  body composition for 12
  carbohydrate replacement during 190
  distances for swimming 2, 94
  drafting rules 162-163
  equipment for 31, 35, 36
  fluid replacement during 190

governing organizations 205
history of v
navigation 57
pacing for 163-164
preswim preparations 172
sources of information on 205, 209,
      211-213, 214
support for swimmers during 9-10
training schedules 118, 123, 130-132
Troup, John 191, 193

U
ultra triathlons 2, 213
undertows 22
United States Olympic Training Center
      (USOTC) 83, 85, 86-89
United States Swimming (USS) 28, 29,
      31, 35, 36, 42-43, 51, 94, 153,
      204
urination 12, 195
U.S. Masters 204
USA National Relay Team 206
USA Triathlon 94, 205

V
Van Dyken, Amy 79
visual imagery 143-144
vitamins 107-108

W
Waikiki Ocean Race 154-155
warm ups 12
water intake 108, 191-193. *See also*
      fluid intake
water starts 156
water temperature 10-14, 20-21. *See
      also* hypothermia
waves 21, 23, 27, 80-81
weather 27-28, 41, 42, 66
Webb, Mathew 24, 189, 210
weight control 108
weight training 97-100, 101, 118
Welch, Greg 164
wet suits 10, 12, 31-33, 216
white boards 183-184
Wilkerson, Jay 28, 210
wind 20, 21, 27, 66
World Championships vi, 68, 153, 160,
      168
World Cup (1990) 44
world-record swims vi, 1, 33-34, 68,
      78, 145, 210-211, 215
World Series Triathlon Corp. (WSTC)
      205
Wrigley Ocean Marathon 197-199

Y
York, John 16
Young, George vi, 198-199, 200, 210

About the Author

A world-record holder in 13 events, Dr. Penny Lee Dean is truly a swimming legend. She has been open water swimming competitively for 30 years, has coached swimming for 22 years, and served 10 years as U.S. National Coach for Open Water Swimming.

Inducted into the International Swimming Hall of Fame in 1996, Dean's list of achievements ranks with the world's best. In 1993, she was named Distinguished Coach by the College Swimming Coaches Association.

In 1978, Dean set the world record for crossing the English Channel, perhaps the sport's most famous event. Her record time of 7 hours, 40 minutes held up for 17 years. Even when her record was broken it was a testament to Dean, as the new record was set by a swimmer she had trained. Dean's time still stands as the fastest by a woman.

In addition, Dean's world-record mark for crossing the Catalina Channel—22 minutes faster than the fastest male swimmer on record—still stands after more than 20 years.

Dean, who holds a doctorate in education, is the women's swimming and water polo coach at the Pomona and Pitzer Colleges (Pomona-Pitzer) in California. She has coached swimming at Pomona-Pitzer for the past 19 years.